DUPLIN COUNTY
North Carolina

Court *of* Pleas &
Quarter Sessions

1803-1805

(Vol. #6)

Abstarcted & Compiled By:
Leora H. McEachern

Please direct all correspondence and orders to:

www.southernhistoricalpress.com
or
SOUTHERN HISTORICAL PRESS, Inc.
PO BOX 1267
Greenville, SC   29601
southernhistoricalpress@gmail.com

ISBN #0-89308-407-7

Printed in the United States of America

18 July 1803   County Court Begun & Held for County of Duplin at the Court House, the 3rd Monday.

Present: Worshipful James Outlaw, Daniel Glisson, James Hall, Joseph Whitfield, Esquires.

Last Will & Testament of Absalom Merritt Exhibited by Nothial Merrit, one of the Ex'rs named in said Will, praying to have it proved & recorded; William Bryant, one of Legatees named in said Will, objected to Probate until he could obtain Council thereon; Court decreed to postpone Probate till next Court.

Tuesday Morning [19 Jul 1803]   Court met a 9 o'clock according to adjournment.

Present: Worshipful James Kenan, Joseph Dickson, Charles Ward, James Outlaw, James Gillespie, Joseph T. Rhodes.

Grand Jury sworn: William McGee, foreman, Isaac Wright, James Lanier, William Hall, Simmion Garner, James Boney, John A. Swinson, John Waller, William Frederick, Jacob Matthis, Lewis Davis, Samuel Bowden, Bazil Kornegay, Jacob Williams, Samuel Davis.

Ordered Jacob Kornegay, Constable, attend Grand Jury.

Appointed Shadrack Stallings, Esq., Timothy Teachy, Esq., & Mesheck Stallings a Committee to act with such Committee as may be or have been appointed by County Court of New Hanover County for viewing & inspecting Bridge over Rockfish Creek between this County & New Hanover County & to contract & agree with workmen to rebuild same & Reporte proceedings to next Court.

Zilphah Byrd, Widow of Benjamin Byrd, dec'd, assigned her right of Administration of her Dec'd Husband Estate to John Hufham, Granted said John Hufham Adm'n of Estate of Benjamin Byrd, dec'd & he gave Bond of £2,000 & took Oath of Adm'r.

Ordered Adm'r of Benjamin Byrd, dec'd, sell Perishable Estate of said dec'd & make return to next Court.

Appointed Jacob Williams, Edward Pearsall, Absalom Best a Committee to divide the Estate of John Williams, dec'd, between Edward Williams & William Williams agreeable to Will of dec'd & return same to next Court.

Ordered William Quinn, Minor Orphan now about 11 the 4th May last, bound Apprentice to John Phillips till age 21 to learn to Read & Write & Cypher & to be a Farmer.

Appointed Temperence Williams Guardian to Edward Williams, Minor Orphan, she gave Bond of £500; Ordered she take his Estate into her possession, etc.

Granted Adm'n of Estate of Lewis Smith to Stephen Smith who gave Bond of £500 & took Oath of Adm'r.

In suit of Rebecka Brock vs Geo. Jernigan Hodom, Sci. Fa. against William Salmon & Jonathan Keithly, Securities for said Rebecka Brock, being executed on them, to show cause etc., said William Salmon & Jonathan Keithly Rendered for Reasons that Execution should not issue against them that there is property in hands of said Rebecka Brock sufficient to discharge costs of said suit; Ordered execution issue against said Rebecka Brock for costs, etc.

Ordered Stephen Smith, Adm'r of Lewis Smith, dec'd, sell Perishable Estate of said dec'd & Return same to next Court.

Appointed Thomas Grimes a constable in room of Lott Stroud, he gave Bond.

Appointed Edward Outlaw a constable in room of Edward Alberson, he gave Bond.

Ordered Sheriff convene a Jury upon the Premises to lay off the Dower of lands of John Woodward, Jr. to his Widow, Catharine Woodward, now Catharine New & reporte same to next Court.

Court proceeded to appointment of a County Surveyor & have by Ballot elected William Beck, Jr.; Ordered Clerk take his Bond of $5,000.

Appointed Thomas Kenedy a constable for one year from this day, he gave Bond.

As Edward Dickson in his lifetime did sell & convey to William Swetman a parcel of land said to be 60 acres but since by examining & ascertaining lines, there appears to be a deficiency of 9 acres, William Swetman, the Purchaser, & Jehu Wilkinson, the Adm'r, have now agreed that the value of said 9 acres shall be settled by Arbitration of such Persons as Court shall appoint; Court Appointed Aaron Williams, Gibson Sloan, John Linton to settle same & ascertain value of said 9 acres & Report their award to next Court.

Court proceeded to elect a Sheriff & elected James Hall, Esq.
for ensuing year; Ordered Clerk certifie same that a Commission may issue.

Ordered Isaac Kornegay, Esq. take list of Taxable Property in
District of Capt. O'Daniels Co. for this year & Return same
to next Court.

Petition from Sundry Inhabitants of this County praying an
Order to turn the Road which now runs through James Matthews
Plantation & make it lead by the new Meeting House, leaving
the old Road at or near Samuel Davis & then a North course
runing between said Meeting House & James Matthews Plantation & into Old Road again at or near Poley Branch; Granted.

Ordered Frederick Graddy, William Alberson, Jonathan Keithly,
James Matthews, James Outlaw, William Roberts, Henry Graddy,
Owen O'Daniel, William Kornegay, Sr., Alexander O'Daniel,
James Bailey, Isaac Kornegay, Daniel Glisson, Jesse Hardy,
Samuel Davis, Edward Outlaw, or any 12 be a Jury to view &
turn said Road agreeable to said Petition & Reporte same to
next Court.

Wednesday Morning [20 Jul 1803] Court met at 9 o'clock according to adjournment.

Present: Worshipful James Kenan, William Beck, Daniel Glisson, Charles Hooks, Esquires.

Granted Adm'n of Estate of Edward Blackmore, dec'd, to Mary
Blackmore, John Hill, Jr. & William Hill jointly who gave
Bond of £10,000 & said John Hill & William Hill have taken
Oath of Adm'rs.

It is further Ordered that Charles Hooks, Esq. shall Admin-
ister Oath of Admin'x to said Mary Blackmore out of Court
& certifie same to Clerk & that Clerk, upon receiving such
certificate shall issue letters accordingly.

Isaac James & Nicanor James, Securities for Arthur Pitmans
Guardianship of the Heirs of John Burton, dec'd, complained
said Guardian is embezeling & waisting Property of said Orphan; Ordered Scitation shall issue said Guardian to appear
at next Court to answer said Complaint & in the mean time, if
it shall appear to satisfaction of William Southerland &
Benjamin Lanier, Esquires, that said property is in danger of
waste or fraud, they take such steps with said Guardian as
may effectually secure same.

Appointed Jehu Wilkinson & William Beck, Jr. Inspecters & Clerks to take the Poll of the Election ensuing to be held in this County for electing a Representative to Congress of the United States.

In suit of Michael Sulliven vs Geo Jernigan Hodom & Ralph Jernigan, this suit was dismissed last Term at Sullivens costs & the other suit against G. J. Hodom, the costs to be agreeable to Jurys verdict notwithstanding the entry that was made last Term of said Judgements of which the Clerk will take due notice in issuing for said costs.

Appointed Isaac Hall Overseer of Road in room of John Balcom, dec'd, & have same District & hands.

Appointed Benjamin Lanier Overseer in room of Jacob Lanier, etc.

Appointed Joseph Thomas Rhodes, John Farrior & William South- erland, Esquires, a Committee to settle the Estate of Byrd Lanier, Esq., dec'd, with Adm'r and to apportion to the Widow her distributive share & Reporte to next Court.

Ordered Adm'rs of Edward Blackmore, dec'd, sell Perishable Estate of said dec'd & make return to next Court.

Appointed Thomas Evens a constable in this County, he gave Bond.

Ordered Thomas Quinn released from his Bond as Guardian of Orphans of James Quinn, dec'd, as said Orphans are taken from him & it appearing to Court that he has none of their prop- erty in his hands.

Appointed Nicanor James Overseer of River in room of George Powell & to have same District & hands & that Daniel Whitman, Isham Larrence & Caner Murray be added to said District & work under him.

Ordered William Hollingsworth and Rueben Nethercut, both in- firm Persons, unable to labour shall in future be exempted from paying a Poll Tax, working on the Road & all other Public Duty.

Ordered Daniel Murray, Overseer of the River, have following hands: Ezekiel Williams, Jonathan Brooks, James Cavenaugh, William Cavenaugh, David Sloan, William Hanchy, Daniel Mur- rays Ben, Arthur Murrays Sam, William Picketts Sam.

In suit of George Powell vs William Cavenaugh, Daniel South- erland & John Hunter, being securities for said William

Cavenaugh, surrendered the Principal & were discharged;
Ordered said William Cavenaugh into custody of Sheriff.

Bond from Mary Whaley to Parish of St. Gabriels to indemnifie
Parish from Maintenance of a Bastard Child Exhibited by Henry
Graddy; Ordered filed.

Ordered Grand Jury have Tickets for two days each this Term.

Hugh McCanne, Esq., Sheriff, rendered his list of Insolvents
for 1802 which Court allowed:

John Grimes	1 Poll
John Irvin	1 Poll
David Cannon	1 Poll
Henry Cannon	1 Poll
Hugh Rhoney	1 Poll
John Armstrong	1 Poll
Duncan Ferguson	1 Poll
Luke Huggins	1 Poll
William Hutson	1 Poll
Anthony Drew	1 Poll
Benjamin Joiner	1 Poll
Henry Hobson	1 Poll
Edwin Whitehead	1 Poll
Bezant Brock	1 Poll
Solomon Blizard	1 Poll
John Rogers	1 Poll
William Stewart	1 Poll
John C. Thomson	1 Poll
Frederick Jones	1 Poll
Joseph Starr	1 Poll
William Smith	1 Poll
John Dale	1 Poll
John Mainor, Jr.	1 Poll
John Hulet	1 Poll
Jesse Brock	1 Poll
Nathan Rouse	1 Poll
Henry Rouse	1 Poll

Ordered list filed.

Ordered Petit Jury have certificates for two days each: Ed
Armstrong, John Hunter, Thomas McGee, John Johnston, William
Pickett, Ben Padget, William Stoakes, Geo. Jernigan Hodom,
Jesse Swinson, Bently Weston.

Appointed Isaac Wright & Joseph Dickson, Jr. Inspecters &
Clerks to take the Poll of ensuing Elections in this County
for a Senator & members of the Commons to the Gen'l Assembly
of the State.

Court decreed & Ordered Clerk shall make no return of any
Person on Tax List to Comptrollers Office for a double Tax
for 1802, Court having satisfactory Reasons for passing this
Order.

Ordered David King shall work on Road under Hezekiah Dobson,
Overseer.

Ordered Jones Smiths Negro Ben work on Road under Bently
Weston, Overseer.

Appointed William Pollock Overseer of Road in room of Thomas
Kenan & have same District & hands.

Appointed Isaac Wright, John Connerly & James Newton Patrollers in District of Capt. Herrings Company.

Thursday Morning [21 Jul 1803] Court met at 9 o'clock according
to adjournment.

Present: Worshipful James Gillespie, Charles Ward, Timothy
Teachey, Esquires.

Reporte of Committee on settlement with Joseph Dickson, Ex'r
of Estate of Robert Dickson, dec'd, with Robert Dickson &
William Dickson, Legatees, by which there appears to be in
hands of said Joseph Dickson a Ballance due Robert Dickson of
£159-9-6 & to William Dickson of £124-11-3; Court concurred
& Ordered recorded.

Inventory of Estate of John Williams, dec'd, Exhibited by
William Williams, Ex'r; Ordered recorded.

Inventory of Estate of Peter Young, dec'd, Exhibited by
Timothy Teachey, Ex'r; Ordered registered [sic].

Inventory of Estate of Isaac Thomas, dec'd, Exhibited by
Lewis Jones, Ex'r; Ordered recorded.

Inventory of Estate of Mary Magdalene Miller, Exhibited by
William Huggins, Adm'r; Ordered Recorded.

Inventory of Estate of John Balcom, dec'd, Exhibited by
Adm'r; Ordered recorded.

Inventory of Estate of John Woodward, Sr., dec'd, Exhibited
by Moses Maning; Ordered recorded.

Account of Sale of Estate of John Woodward, Sr., dec'd,
Exhibited by Moses Maning, Adm'r; Ordered recorded.

Account of Sale of Estate of Bird Lanier, dec'd, Exhibited by
Ben Lanier, Adm'r; Ordered recorded.

Account of Sale of Estate of Isaac Thomas, dec'd, Exhibited
by Lewis Jones, Ex'r.; Ordered recorded.

Additional Account of Sale of Estate of Lewis Thomas, dec'd,
Exhibited by James Reardon, Ex'r; Ordered recorded.

Account of Sale of Estate of Thomas Hooks, dec'd, Exhibited;
Ordered recorded.

Allowed Hugh McCanne, Sheriff, £7-14-0, the amount of a Jury
Ticket issued George Houston in 1801, out of County Tax for
1802, said Ticket having been lost by Moses Maning.

Appointed William Southerland, James Hall, Jehu Wilkinson a
Committee to settle the accounts of the Estate of Amos
Johnston with Nathan Waller, Ex'r & Reporte same to next
Court.

Deed of Gift: Elizabeth Halso to Lindy Halso for sundries,
proved by James Lanier; Ordered registered.

Power of Attorney: Josiah Stafford to William Alberson,
proved by Durham Graddy; Ordered registered.

Bill of Sale: Jacob Matthis to John Matthis for a Negro girl
Easter, proved by Elijah Tucker; Ordered registered.

Bill of Sale: Uriah Bass to Willis Hines for a Negro woman
Hobb, proved by Lewis Herring; Ordered registered.

Bill of Sale: Dennis & David Cannon to Auston Beasley for a
Negro girl Mary, proved by Jacob Matthis; Ordered registered.

Bill of Sale: Shadrack Stallings to Joshua Blake for a Negro
Judy, Acknowledged; Ordered registered.

Deed of Gift: Michael Dickson to his son Abishai Dickson for
a Negro girl Patty, Acknowledged; Ordered registered.

Deed of Gift: William Graddy to John & Charity Outlaw for a
Negro girl Chaney, proved by John A. Swinson; Ordered registered.

Deed [of Gift?]: William Graddy to Timothy Graddy for a
Negro man Sam, proved by John A. Swinson; Ordered registered.

Deed of Gift: William Graddy to Lewis Graddy for a Negro man Bob, proved by John A. Swinson; Ordered registered.

Deed of Gift: William Graddy to Henry Graddy for a Negro man Toney, proved by John A. Swinson; Ordered registered.

Deed of Gift: William Graddy to Frederick Graddy for a Negro woman Biner, proved by John A. Swinson; Ordered registered.

Deed of Gift: William Graddy to Joseph Whitfield & Wife for a Negro girl Hanah, proved by John A. Swinson; Ordered registered.

Deed: Mary Murdock to William McGee for 60 acres, proved by Joseph Dickson; Ordered registered.

Deed: Caleb Quin to Jesse Harris for 200 acres, proved by Nathan Waller; Ordered registered.

Deed: Joseph Dickson to George Powell for 76 acres, Acknowledged; Ordered registered.

Deed: William Alberson to Joseph Green for sundry parcels of land, proved by David Herring; Ordered registered.

Deed: James Murray to Nicanor James for 120 acres, proved by Thomas Evens; Ordered registered.

Deed: Jonathan Thomas to William Boyet for 75 acres, proved by Charles Hooks; Ordered registered.

Deed: James Boney to Meshack Stallings for 39 acres, Acknowledged; Ordered registered.

Deed: William McCanne, Jr. to George Powell for 200 acres, proved by Joseph Dickson; Ordered registered.

Deed: John Byrd to Matthew Branch for 71 acres, proved by Charles Hooks; Ordered registered.

Deed: James Lanier to Snowdon Pearse for 200 acres, proved by Moses Maning; Ordered registered.

Deed: Hogan Hunter to Isaac Midleton for 150 acres, Acknowledged; Ordered registered.

Deed: Jacob Boney to John McGowen for 170 acres, proved by Timothy Teachey; Ordered registered.

Deed: Martin Hanchy to David Sloan for 126 acres, proved by Aaron Williams; Ordered registered.

Deed: John Williams to Benjamin Williams for 200 acres, proved by Tim. Teachey; Ordered registered.

Deed: John Goff, Sr. To Augustin Jones for 71 acres, proved by John Matthis; Ordered registered.

Deed: Thomas Johnston to William Boyet for 100 acres, proved by Jonathan Thomas; Ordered registered.

Deed: Jonathan Thomas to Edw'd Blackmore for 64 acres, Acknowledged; Ordered registered.

Deed: Arthur Boyet to Edward Blackmore for 45 acres, proved by Jonathan Thomas; Ordered registered.

Deed: James Outlaw to John Outlaw for 340 acres, Acknowledged; Ordered registered.

Deed: James Outlaw to Edward Outlaw for 300 acres, Acknowledged; Ordered registered.

Reporte of the Committee appointed to settle accounts of Estate of Thomas Molten, a Minor, with Andrew McIntire, his Guardian, by which it appears a ballance of Estate of said Thomas Molten in hands of said Guardian is £131-18-2; Court concurred & Ordered registered.

Ordered Sarah Lanier, wife of Jesse Lanier, dec'd, allowed for maintinance of one of his children, called Sarah, for one year from this date, the sum of £12-10-0 to be taken out of distributive share of its dec'd fathers Estate.

Grand Jury Reported several Orphan Children suffering for want of attention of Court: William Jones, son of Charity Jones; James, son of Charity Benton; Rachel Johnston in care of Nancy Henderson; three girls, Orphans of Robert Miller, dec'd; Scott, Orphan of Joseph Bray, dec'd; Ordered Clerk issue notice to Sheriff that he cause said Children be convened before next Court that they may be provided for.

Allowed Moses Maning 24 shillings for attending Court three days this Term as constable.

Allowed Jacob Kornegay 16 shillings for attending Court as constable two days this Term.

<u>Friday Morning [22 Jul 1803]</u>   Court met at 9 o'clock according
   to adjournment.

   Present: Worshipful Joseph Dickson, James Gillespie, Edward
   Pearsall, James Dickson, William Southerland.

   James Hall, Esq., produced a Commission from the Governor
   under his hand & Seal of the State bearing date 21 of this
   Instant July, 1803, appointing his Sheriff of said County of
   Duplin for one year to commence from this Term, whereupon the
   said James Hall gave Bond as Sheriff & County Treasurer &
   took Oaths for Qualification of Officers & Sheriff.

   Bill of Sale: John Houston to William Hall for a Negro man
   Dick, proved by James Hall; Ordered registered.

   Appointed Edward Pearsall, Jr. & William Mizzell Patrollers
   for lower end of Capt. Pearsalls Co.

   Jurors appointed to serve at next Court are: David Wright,
   John Connerly, Thomas Hill, Stephen B. Herring, James Biz-
   zell, James Watkins, Joseph Dickson, Jr., James Grimes, Heze-
   kiah Millard, Lot Stroud, Alexander O'Daniel, John Outlaw,
   Henry Graddy, Edward Albertson, Jacob Lanier, Nathan Will-
   iams, Joseph Screws, Joab Fountain, Phill Southerland, Jr.,
   Tobias Southerland, Auston Bryan, Jesse Brown, John Houston,
   Richard Swinson, Lewis Barfield, Jr., David Midleton, Hogan
   Hunter, William McGowen, Richard Norment, Obadiah Wade,
   Elijah Mallard, Jeremiah Pearsall, Joseph Grimes, Howell
   Best, Wm Waterman, Mesheck Stallings, Daniel Murphy, John
   Boney, Henry Allen, Thomas Wells, William Swetman, Joseph
   Williams, Jr., Hardy Carleton.

   It being represented to Court that the present situation of
   Charles Goff, a blind man now under Guardianship of Court,
   renders him incapable of paying due attention to his family,
   Ordered John Goff, son of said Charles Goff, now age 19, be
   Bound Apprentice to James Thomas Rhodes till age 21 to learn
   trade of Cart Wheel & Waggon maker.

   Court Adjourned Till Court in Course.

   [signed] Jam's Gillespie, Edw'd Pearsall, James Dickson,
   W. Southerland.

<u>17 October 1803</u>   County Court Begun & Held for County of Duplin
at the Court House, the 3rd Monday.

Present: Worshipful James Outlaw, William Beck, Charles
Hooks, Edward Pearsall, Esquires.

Bill of Sale: David Wright to Archibald McCalop for a Negro
woman Elinor & child Emery, Acknowledged; Ordered registered.

Appointed William Beck, Edward Pearsall, Charles Hicks,
Esquires, as a Committee to settle the Estate of Thomas
Norment, dec'd, with Ex'rs & Reporte to this Court.

Inventory of Estate of Edward Blackmore Exhibited by William
Hill, one of the Adm'rs; Ordered recorded.

Account of Sale of Estate of Edward Blackmore, dec'd, Exhibited by William Hill, one of the Adm'r; Ordered recorded.

<u>Tuesday Morning [18 Oct 1803]</u> Court met at 10 O'clock according
to adjournment.

Present: Worshipfull James Kenan, Robert Southerland, William Beck, James Pearsall, Edward Pearsall, Daniel Glisson,
Esquires.

List of Grand Jury: David Wright, Joseph Grimes, Jeremiah
Pearsall, Rec'd his Ticket, Thomas Wells, John Outlaw, Alex'r
O'Daniel, Howel Best, Joseph Screws, received his Ticket,
Phill Southerland, Jr., Hogan Hunter, David Midleton, Elijah
Mallard, Tobias Southerland
[two lines illegible].

Deed: Benj'n & Jacob Lanear to John Holden for 100 acres,
proved by Andrew McIntire; Ordered registered.

Granted Martha Bell Adm'n of Estate of her dec'd husband
Hezekiah Bell.

Appointed James Newton Overseer in place of Maurice Moore &
to have same hands & District.

Deed: James Bailey to Jonathan Keathly for 578 acres, proved
by Durham Graddy; Ordered registered.

Deed: Joseph Williams to Simeon Wood for 35 [or 75] acres,
proved by David Williams; Ordered registered.

Appointed William Burnham, Jr. Guardian to Senea Hedlet[?] & to give Bond of $1,000, or more properly £500.

["Inventory & Account of Sales of Estate of Benjamin Byrd returned by John Hufham, Adm'r. Bond Not Given" marked through.]

Petit Jury sworn: Thomas Hill, Stephen B. Herring, Edward Albertson, Austen Bryan, William Swetman, Joseph Williams, Hardy Carleton, Henry Graddy, Henry Allen, Robert Besshop, James Watkins, David Hooks.

Ordered John Wilkinson, Theophilus Guy & Daniel L. Kenan, who agreeable to a certificate assigned by James Kenan one of the Justices of the Peace for County of Duplin, Qualified as Patrollers for Capt. Herrings District, be allowed 40 shillings for extra services during 1802.

As Martha Bell having Qualified as Adm'x of Estate of her dec'd husband, Hezekiah Bell, & having rec'd letters of Adm'n, Ordered she sell all perishable property of Estate of her dec'd husband & Reporte an inventory & Account of Sales.

Deed: Henry Cook, Ezekiel Dunkin, Jain Dunkin, Henry Hulet & Mary Hulet to William Carr for 250 acres proved by John Bryan; Ordered registered.

Ordered Jacob Boney, Jacob Wells & Timothy Teachy be a Committee to divide the Estate of Peter Young, dec'd, agreeable to Will & Reporte to next Court.

Allowed Mary Futch 10 shillings for each month for 16 months for nursing a Bastard Child & Execution be issued against Stephen Gibbons, father of said Child for same.

Appointed Moses Stanley Guardian to Robert Peal, he offers for Security Daniel Glisson, Esq. & Joseph Whitfield, Esq. & gave Bond of £500; Ordered he take property of said Peal into his possession.

Ordered Samuel Houston be Overseer of Road in room of George Houston & have same District & hands.

Ordered John Halso be Overseer of Road in room of Benja Lenear & have same hands & District.

As a Petition has been presented signed by sundry Inhabitants of Muddy Creek praying the opening of a Road from Road leading from James Picketts landing to New River, Ordered following appointed Jurors to lay off said New Road & report a correct Plan thereof when done: Archibald Thomas, John

Walder, William Bazden, Nathan Walder, Joseph Thomas Rhodes,
Jesse Brown, Charles Bostwic, Samuel Bostwic, Isaac Whaily,
Job Hunter, Benjamin Padget, Meret Manning, Moses Manning,
Robert Harriss, Robert Bishop, Abner Cottle, Hicks Mills,
John Thigpen; Ordered Moses Manning, Constable, summon &
convene aforesaid to act as Jurors or any 12 & they report a
plan as above directed to next Court.

Upon motion of Robert Southerland Ordered Nathan Walder &
Jesse Brown be & are appointed Patrollers in Capt. Browns Co.
& they apply to some Magistrate & take Oath.

Account of Sales of Estate of John Balkcum returned by James
Mathews, Adm'r; Ordered recorded.

As William Beck, Edward Pearsall & Charles Hooks, Esq'rs,
being appointed a Committee to examine accounts & papers in
any way appertaining to Estate of Thomas Normant Exhibited by
Ex'r & Report as follows: We the Subscribers being appointed
a Committee to settle the accounts of the Estate of Thomas
Normant, dec'd, with Executors to his Will have proceeded to
examine the vouchers in the hands of said Executors & find to
the amount of £1507-11-3 1/2, but no settlement can be made
as the whole of the debts are not paid, all of which is now
submitted to the Worshipful Court now sitting; October 18th,
1803, signed William Beck, Edward Pearsall, Charles Hooks.

Ordered Stephen Miller is authorized to continue & improve a
Mill which he has begun on his own land across Maple Swamp
without any public interference thereto.

Appointed William Pickett, Jr. Overseer in place of James
Williams, to work same hands including Robert Coal & likewise
same District.

Allowed Jesse George 40 shillings for services as Patroller
in Capt. Kerrs Co.

Deed: Jonathan Davis, Sr. To Jonathan Davis, Jr. for 200
acres, proved by John Green; Ordered registered.

Deed: John Green to Timothy Green for 180 acres, proved by
David Williams; Ordered registered.

Deed: John Goff, Sr. to Abraham Newton for 150 acres, proved
by John Lee; Ordered registered.

Deed: Joshua Byrd to Michael Byrd for 100 acres, proved by
James Bowden; Ordered registered.

Deed: Richard Blanton to Sam'l Davis for 69 acres, proved by
Timothy Teachy; Ordered registered.

Deed: James Williams to William Sowell for 20 acres, proved by Robert Southerland; Ordered registered.

Deed: Isaah Rogers to Andrew Gufford for 150 acres, Acknowledged; Ordered registered.

Deed of Gift: John Green, Sr. to John Green, Jr. for 190 acres, Acknowledged; Ordered registered.

Deed of Gift: Samuel Albertson to Sarah Albertson for 100 acres in one tract & 197 in a second & in a third 100, Acknowledged; Ordered registered.

Deed: Isaac James to Samuel Webb for 20 acres, Acknowledged; Ordered registered.

Deed: Hugh McCanne, Sheriff to Lincoln Shuffield for 12 acres, Acknowledged; Ordered registered.

Deed: Luke Mazell to William Mazell for 80 acres, Acknowledged; Ordered registered.

Deed of Gift: Jonathan Davis to his son Samuel Davis for 100 acres, proved by John Green; Ordered registered.

Deed: John Wilkings to Nehemiah Forehand for 100 acres, proved by Jesse Forehand; Ordered registered.

Deed: George Thomas to Solomon Carter for 85 acres, proved by Christopher Lawson; Ordered registered.

Deed: Joseph Williams, Sr. to Simon Wood for 75 acres, proved by David Williams; Ordered registered.

Deed: Joseph Williams, Jr. to David Williams for 50 acres, proved by Joseph Williams; Ordered registered.

Deed: James Bailey to Jonathan Keathly for 578 acres, proved by Durham Graddy; Ordered registered.

Deed: Frederick Williams to David Williams for 90 acres, proved by Joseph Williams; Ordered registered.

Deed: John Brown to David Williams for 50 acres, proved by Joseph Williams; Ordered registered.

Deed: Meshack Stallings to Daniel Wood for 100 acres, proved by Shadrack Stallings; Ordered registered.

Inventory & account of Sales of property of Benjamin Byrd, dec'd, returned by John Hufham, Adm'r.

Account of sales of property of Estate of Lewis[?] Smith,
dec'd, returned by Stephen Smith, Adm'r.

Bill of Sale: Page Jernigan & David Slocumb of Wayne Co. to
Felix Kenan Hill of Duplin Co. for a Negro girl Lucy, proved
by James Clark; Ordered registered.

Deed of Gift: Jesse Harriss & Nathan Walder to Caleb Quin
conveying their rights to a Negro girl Venus formerly property of Amos Johnson, dec'd, Acknowledged; Ordered registered.

Bill of Sale: Abraham Kornegay, Sr. of Jones Co. to Bazil
Kornegay for a Negro woman Rose, proved by Bryan Kornegay;
Ordered registered.

Bill of Sale: William Mazell to Luke Mazell for a Negro boy
Frank, proved by Mark Mazell; Ordered registered.

Bill of Sale: Owen O'Daniel to Stephen Herring for his right
to a Negro woman Phoebe, proved by James Rafield; Ordered
registered.

Bill of Sale: Hollowell Tatom to Joseph Smith for a Negro
girl Phillis, proved by Jacob Williams (Maple).

As Gibson Sloan, John Linton & Aaron Williams being appointed
to arbitrate a matter of controversy between William Swetman
& Dr. Jehu Wilkinson, Adm'r of Estate of Edward Dickson,
dec'd, relative to a piece of land sold by said Dickson &
said to contain 60 acres but on surveying was found to be a
deficiency of 9 acres, they do Order the said William Swetman
shall receive from Adm'r £10 which is amount of valuation of
above mentioned deficiency.

[No day given, apparently Wednesday, 19 Oct 1803] Court met at
10 o'clock according to adjournment.

Present: Worshipful James Kenan, James Maxwell, Daniel Glisson, William Duncan

Appointed Austen Bryan Overseer in place of James Wallace &
to have same hands & District with addition of Rueben &
Thomas Cottle who properly belong to same District.

Appointed William W. Pollock Guardian of Bedee Merit & McKen-
zie Merit; Ordered he take said Children of Absalom Meret
under his care & that he give Bond of £500; he offers as
security Thomas Kenan.

Allowed William Kornegay 40 shillings for serving as Patroller in Capt. Daniels District in 1802.

Allowed George Powell 40 shillings for service as Patroller in Capt. Kerrs District.

Ordered William Pickett, Jr. cleared from doing any Public labor on Road or River until he shall recover, he now has an inflamation in his leg.

Ordered William Kornegay be Overseer in place of Alexander Graddy to work same hands & District.

Ordered John Farior, Robert Southerland, William Pickett be a Committee to settle accounts of Estate of John Burton with Adm'r & Report to next Court.

As William Frederick, Constable, presented to Court which was received, a report of following named Jurors appointed to lay off a New Road beginning at James Wrights gates & crossing Bearswamp at William Guys & thence joining Old Road near Sam'l Stanfords being more particularly described in the Report: Felix K. Hill, Wm. Bennet, Jo Dickson, John Guy, D'l Kenan, Wm. Dickson, Wm. Beck, Cullin Connerly, Felix Frederick, Wm. Branch, James Wright, David Wright; Aforesaid Jurors having been convened by said Constable & proceeded pursuant to Order, Allowed said Constable, Wm. Frederick, 2/8 for each acting Juror, say no. 12 for his services.

Allowed Jeremiah Pearsall 40 shillings for service as Patroller for 1802 in Edward Pearsalls Co.

Ordered Sheriff to summon a Jury who with himself shall allot to Mary Blackmore, widow of Edward Blackmore, dec'd, a third part of personal Estate of which said Edward died possessed.

Report of Committee to divide the Estate of John Williams, dec'd, between William Williams & Edward Williams, returned by Edward Pearsall; Ordered filed: William Williams - £35-5-0, Edward Williams - £35-5-0.

Ordered Temperance Williams, Guardian to Edward Williams, sell at six months credit that part of perishable Estate of said Orphans which was laid off to him from Estate of John Williams, dec'd.

Isaac Kornegay, upon application of William Albertson, is appointed Overseer to work on River in place of William Albertson with same hands & District, adding hereto the following: Isaac Kornegays hands, Sam'l Smiths & Alexander Graddys Peter.

["Ordered Lucretia Weston, Orphan, Bound to Suthy Raphell &
it is required of said Suthy Raphell to learn the above named
& bounden to read the Bible to sew & nit" marked through.]
Note the parties disappeared therefore the entry left
["incomplete" marked through] unperfect.

Ordered David Williams, Abraham Newton, John Hufham be a
Committee to lay off to Martha Bell one years provisions out
of perishable property of her dec'd husband & return report
to next Court.

Allowed Mary Williford £13 out of goods & lands of Stephen
Gibbons & Clerk issue execution accordingly.

Appointed William Williams a constable in Capt. Pearsalls Co.
in place of Charles Williamson, he gave Bond with Benjamin
Best & Jacob Williams (Maple) as securities.

Appointed Solomon Jones Overseer of Road in room of Lewis
Grimes & to have same hands & District.

Allowed Thomas Evans 8 shillings per day for two days attendance as constable this Court.

Allowed Love Savage, Constable, 8 shillings per day for two
days attendance on the Court.

Appointed Superior Court Jurors: William Albertson, John
Stallings, James Murray, Moses Manning, John F. Rhodes,
Thomas McGee, Thomas Garrison.

Allowed Andrew Hewit[?], Peter Frederick & Isham Faison
40 shillings for services as Patrollers in Capt. Herrings
District.

Ordered Sampson Grimes, Lewis Herring, Esquires, take depo-
sition of William Graddy & Forward same to next Court to be
read in evidence in behalf of State against James & Alexander
Outlaw.

Appointed Gen'l James Kenan, Andrew McIntire, David Midleton
& David Wright to allot to Mary Blackmore, widow of late
Edward Blackmore, a necessary part of the crop, stock &
provisions for support of herself & family for term of one
year.

Ordered Jehu Wilkinson, Andrew McIntire, James Hall be a
Committee to settle accounts of Edward Pearsall as Guardian
to John J. Middleton & Reporte same to next Court.

Ordered following serve as Jurors at next Court: Jacob
Williams, William Waterman, Andrew Stokes, John Best,

David Davis, Stephen Williams, William Stokes, Lewis Carlton,
William Frederick, Richard Norman, Jehu Wilkinson, Joseph
Gillespie, William Hall, Jr., Isaac Middleton, Robert Bis-
hop[?], Benjamin Delany, Henry Newkirk, Abner Cottle, Jona-
than Keithly, Stephen Herring, Mill, Oen O'Daniel, Benjamin
Herring, Isom Faison, John Byrd, James Price, James Ward,
Samuel Houston, Richard Swinson, Lewis Barfield, Daniel
Murphy, John Boney, William Carr, John Thally, James Grimes,
Edward Winders, Moses Stanley, Zach Turnage, John Beck, Bazel
Kornega, Joseph Dickson, James Johnston, Nathan Williams,
Merit Maning, James Lanier.

[No day given, apparently Thursday, 20 Oct 1803] Court met at
10 o'clock according to adjournment.

Present: Worshipful Charles Ward, Edward Pearsall

Court adjourned.

[No day given, apparently Friday, 21 Oct 1803] Court met at 10
o'clock according to adjournment.

Present: Worshipful James Wright, Edward Pearsall, Hugh
McCann, James Maxwell, Esquires.

Ordered Margaret Maxwell, Adm'x to Henry Maxwell her dec'd
husband, be directed by Sheriff to come to next Court to
settle Estate of dec'd with said Court.

Ordered Hugh McCann be Overseer of Road from Lincoln Shuf-
fields Landing to middle of Maxwell at Chastens ford & have
following hands [added?] to it: Nathan'l McCanns & Hugh
McCanns hands, Henry Cook, William Cook, Jacob Parker.

Bound Mary Ann Johnston Apprentice to James Pickette till age
18, to learn to read the Bible, Spin, nit & weave.

Ordered Emanuel Knowles work on River under William McCann.

Court Adjourned Till Court in Course.

[signed] J. Pearsall, W. Southerland, Ja's Maxwell, B.
Bowden

Deed: Archibald Carr to John Johnston for 137 acres, proved by Edward Pearsall; Ordered registered.

Deed: Archibald Carr to John Johnston for 120 acres, proved by Edward Pearsall; Ordered registered.

Deed: John Johnston to Elisabeth Johnston for 300 acres, Acknowledged; Ordered registered.

Deed: Thomas Routledge to Edward Pearsall for 200 acres, proved by John Johnston; Ordered registered.

Deed: Archibald Carr to Edward Pearsall for 80 acres, proved by James Pearsall; Ordered registered.

Deed: John Hill to Edward Pearsall for 265 acres, proved by James Pearsall; Ordered registered.

Deed: John Johnston to Edward Pearsall for 300 acres, Acknowledged; Ordered registered.

James Hall, Esq., returned his List of Taxables.

Charles Hooks, Esq., returned his list of Taxables.

Edward Pearsall, Esq., returned his List of Taxables.

Joseph Whitfield, Esq., returned his list of Taxables.

Isaac Kornegay, Esq., returned his list of Taxables.

Jacob Williams, Esq., returned his list of Taxables.

W. Southerland, Esq., returned his list of Taxables.

John Farrior, Esq., returned his list of Taxables.

Tim Teachey, Esq., returned his list of Taxables.

Gibson Sloan, Esq., returned his list of Taxables.

Bryan Bowden, Esq., returned his list of Taxables.

Inventory of Estate of Benjamin Byrd, dec'd, Exhibited by John Hufham, Adm'r; Ordered recorded.

Account of Sale of Estate of Benjamin Byrd, dec'd, Exhibited by John Hufham; Ordered recorded.

Account of Sale of Estate of Lewis Smith, dec'd, Exhibited by
Stephen Smith, Adm'r; Ordered recorded.

James Branch, charged with begeting a Bastard Child of Mary
Present, a single woman, gave bond required by Law.

Appointed Jacob Kornegay, William Williams, William Glisson &
Thomas Evens constables in this County for one year; each
gave Bond.

<u>16 January 1804</u>   County Court Begun & Held for County of Duplin
at the Court House, the third Monday.

Present: Worshipful James Outlaw, James Pearsall, Daniel
Glisson, Edward Pearsall, Esquires.

Court Adjourned.

<u>Tuesday Morning [17 Jan 1804]</u>   Court met at 10 o'clock accord-
ing to adjournment.

Present: Worshipful James Outlaw, James Pearsall, Daniel
Glisson, Edward Pearsall, Esquires.

Receipt from Heirs of William Best, dec'd, to William Frederick, Ex'r, Exhibited by William Frederick; Ordered recorded
& is as follows: We & each of us do acknowledge to have
received of William Frederick, Ex'r to our Fathers last Will
& Testament, our full & proportionable share of his Estate
which he died seized and possessed of, We say received by us
in full this 4th day of January 1804. John Best, William
Best, Mary her X mark Best, Elizabeth X Best.

Reporte of the Committee to allot & lay off to Mary Blackmore, Widow of Edward Blackmore, dec'd, provisions, etc. for
one year was rendered; Court concurred & Ordered recorded as
follows: 80 barrels corn, 3,000 lbs pork, 8 stacks Blades &
all the top stacks on the Manor Plantation & one good Beef,
30 bushels Potato slips & all the Potatoes & 10 bushel Peas.

Reporte of Dower of Edward Blackmore land laid off for Mary
Blackmore, Widow of dec'd, Rendered by Sheriff; Court concurred & Ordered recorded.

Grand Jury sworn: Jehu Wilkinson, foreman, William Fred-
erick, Sr., Owen O'Daniel, Stephen Herring (M), Jonathan
Keithly, Jo Gillespie, Isaac Midleton, Andrew Stoakes,
Richard Norment, Henry Newkirk, Jacob Williams, Lewis
Barfield Jr., William Waterman.

Ordered Peleg Rogers, Constable, attend Grand Jury.

Appointed Henry Fountain Overseer of Road in room of James
Batts, to have same District & hands.

Granted Bridget Ward, Widow & Ex'r of Luke Ward, dec'd, an
Order to sell Perishable part of Property of said dec'd's
Estate in her possession & make return to next Court.

Appointed Lewis Jones Overseer of Road in room of Reading Bowden, to have same District & hands.

Appointed Francis Oliver, James Reardon & David Wright a Committee to divide the lands of the late Thomas Hooks, dec'd, between Susana Hooks, widow of said Thomas Hooks, and David Hooks, son of said Thomas Hooks agreeable to Will of said dec'd & make return to next Court.

Mary Quinn, Widow of James Quinn, dec'd, prayed an allowance for maintaining her five children to this present time; Court allowed her £10 for same to be paid out of her dec'd husbands Estate by Adm'rs.

Appointed Shadrack Stallings, John Matthis, David Hall a Committee to lay off Dower of lands of late John Balcom, dec'd, to Heater Balcomb, Widow of dec'd, & return same to next Court.

Appointed Thomas Kenan, Isaac Wright & Benjamin Best a Committee to settle accounts of Estate of Nathan Boyet, dec'd, with John Fleming, Adm'r & return thereof to next Court.

Appointed Joseph Whitfield, Bazil Kornegay, Wm Duncan, John Kornegay, & Jacob Kornegay a Committee to divide lands & Negroes of David Peal, dec'd, among the four heirs claiming the same & return same to next Court.

Appointed Hillary Peale Guardian to William Peale, a Minor, he gave Bond of £500; Ordered he take his Estate into his Possession.

Appointed David Durell Overseer of Road in room of Moses Stanley to have same District & hands.

["Appointed William Brown Overseer of Road in room of Hardy Carleton to have same District & hands" marked through.]

Philip Coley, charged with begeting a Bastard Child of Sally Matthis, gave Bond required by Law.

Wednesday Morning [18 Jan 1804]   Court met at 9 o'clock according to adjournment.

Present: Worshipful James Kenan, James Dickson, Shadrack Stallings, William Beck, James Wright, Hugh McCanne, Edward Pearsall, James Maxwell, Esquires.

Appointed Solomon Jones Overseer of Road & his District to be
as formerly & have hands below the Great Path from head of
Halls Marsh by a place known as the Cowper house to Old Road,
thence down said Old Road opposite head of Bearakin Branch,
thence down said branch to Goshen Swamp, thence down said
Swamp to Col. Wards Bridge, including the hands therein &
also Hampton Sulliven & William Benton are ad[d]ed to said
District.

Allowed Henry Cannon 40 shillings for serving as Patroller
last year, 1803.

John Winders suggested there was an error in his Patent for
200 acres in Duplin on Goshen Swamp dated 22 Nov. 1771 [No.]
348; Ordered County Surveyor inspect same & reports thereon
to this Court. Pursuant to which Order County Surveyor,
William Beck, reported the Course in said Patent which says
S 50 W 200 pole, ought to say S 50 E 200 pole which will
agree with survey; Ordered Clerk certifie same.

Power of Attorney: Sarah Liddon of Davidson County, Tenn. to
William Barfield Exhibited & appears to have been recorded in
Davidson County, Tenn & duly executed there & properly attested by Clerk of said County Court, also is accompanied by
a certificate from James Robertson, Presiding Justice of the
Peace in said Davidson County; Ordered Power of Attorney &
certificates registered.

Allowed Durham Graddy 40 shillings for serving as Patroller
last year, 1803.

[Granted] John Farrior, Adm'r of Ebenezer Garrison, dec'd, an
Order to sell a Negro of said dec'ds Estate named Peg in
order to raise money to pay off James Garrison his distributive share of said Estate & reports to next Court.

Appointed Joseph Thomas Rhodes, William Southerland, Henry
Newkirk a Committee to settle accounts of Estate of Ebenezer
Garrison, dec'd, with John Farrior, Adm'r & to ascertain the
share of James Garrison, one of the Claimants & return thereof to next Court.

Appointed William Brown Overseer of Road in room of Hardy
Carleton from Stewarts Creek at County line down to John
Williams & have following hands: Jacob Matthis, Jr., William
Matthis, Auston Beesley, Archibald Cook, Hansel Ezell, Gab-
riel Merrit, William Merrit, Jr., Elias Sutton, Ezekiel
Matthis, John Vann, William Watson, John Crumpton, Thomas
Lanier, Timothy Murphy, William Swetman, Hardy Carleton.

Allowed Robert Midleton & John Phillips 40 shillings each for serving as Patrollers last year, 1803.

Allowed Edward McGowen & James Frederick 40 shillings each for serving as Patrollers last year, 1803.

David Davis recorded his mark, a smooth crop in each ear & a slit in the left ear.

Appointed James Dickson, Sr. adm'r of Estate of James Quin, dec'd, in stead of Benjamin Beat the Adm'r who has resigned & the said James Dickson has given Bond of £500.

Appointed Hugh McCanne, William McCanne & Jehu Wilkinson a Committee to settle accounts of Estate of Henry Maxwell, dec'd, with Adm'x & ascertain the amount of said Estate in hands of said Adm'x & make an equal division of same between the two children & Widow of said dec'd & Reporte to next Court.

Allowed John Hunter 40 shillings for serving as Patroller for 1800.

Appointed Jehu Wilkinson, David Midleton & Isaac Midleton a Committee to settle the accounts of the Estate of James Quinn, dec'd, with Benjamin Beat the late Adm'r & make return to next Court.

Allowed Jurors who were convened & served in laying off Dower, etc. for Mary Blackmore, two days each, 8 shillings per day & that Clerk issue certificates for same.

Appointed Shadrack Stallings, Gibson Sloan & William Stoaks to settle accounts of Estate of Barbara Murphy, dec'd, with Frederick Wells, Ex'r & reporte same to next Court.

Appointed Jonathan Keathly Overseer of Road in room of Alexander Keaton & have same District & hands.

Continued James Dickson Overseer of Road as formerly from Grove to Maxwell.

Appointed David Wilkins Overseer of Road in room of James Rhodes & have same District & hands.

Ordered Tax of 2 shillings on each & every Poll & on each & every 300 acres in this County levied & collected for 1803 for County contingences.

Also Tax of 6 pence on each & every Poll & each & every 300 acres in this County for 1803 for building a Bridge over the NorthEast River at mouth of Limestone Creek.

Granted John Waller a Licence to keep a Public Tavern or Victualing house where he now lives on the New River Road at Limestone Swamp in this County, he offers as Securities James Dickson & Jacob Williams; Ordered Clerk take Bond & make out License; Rec'd 48 shillings, the Clerks fee & State Tax.

Allowed John Cooper, Hogan Hunter 40 shillings each for serving as Patrollers for 1802.

As sundry Judgements have heretofore been obtained by sundry Persons against Jerediah B. Foley & executions thereon have been levied on land of said Jerediah B. Foley which land is claimed & sale forbidden by Stephen Jones, etc.; Ordered Sheriff summon a Jury of good & lawful freeholders according to Law to try the Property of said land so levied upon & proceed thereon as Law in such case directs.

Appointed Jacob Williams, Edward Pearsall, Jr. be Patrollers for lower part of District of Capt. Pearsalls Co. for ensuing year.

Appointed William Beck, Edward Pearsall & Charles Hooks a Committee to settle accounts of Estate of Thomas Normant, dec'd, with Ex'rs & Reporte to next Court.

["Jehu Wilkinson, Andrew McIntire & James Hall are appointed a Committee to settle accounts of Edward Pearsall, Guardian to John J. Midleton & Reporte to next Court" marked through.]

Allowed Jeremiah Pearsall 40 shillings for serving as Patroller for 1802.

Appointed Jacob Brown, Jr. Overseer of Road from the Flag Pond to Farriors Foard on Muddy Creek in room of James Pickett & have same District & hands.

Appointed Thomas Cole Overseer of Road in room of William Pickett on Road leading from James Picketts landing to the Meeting House, called the New River Road, & have same District & hands.

Ordered Mary James, Widow, be exhonerated from payment of Tax for her Negro woman Harriet for 1799, 1800, 1801 & 1802 & that Sheriff be allowed same with County Trustees for 1802.

Charles Hooks, Guardian to Thomas Ivey, Orphan, is exonerated from his Bond as Guardian to said Thomas Ivey & is hereby

directed to give up the property of said Orphan to said
Thomas Ivey.

James Clark is also exonerated from his Indentures which he
gave when said Orphan, Thomas Ivey, was bound to him.

Allowed Benjamin Best & Jonathan Thomas 40 shillings each for
serving as Patrollers for 1803.

Pursuant to an Order of last October Term a Jury has been
convened upon the premises to lay off a New Road leading from
James Picketts landing to New River, to County line of Jones
County on the way to the Road leading from Limestone to New
Bern at or near John Stels Shop, have proceeded as follows:
Beginning at first mentioned Road from Picketts landing to
Onslow, the fork near Staffords Swamp Meeting House, running
a direct line about 1/2 mile crossing a small branch, thence
a direct line between Benjamin Padgets & Isaac Padgets set-
tlements & between William & Edward Hunters to Muddy Creek at
Hunters foard, thence a direct line to Jesse Browns foard on
Stephens Swamp, thence by the east end of Jesse Browns home
Plantation to the west end of his other Plantation commonly
called the Woodward field, thence a direct line to Batch-
elders Swamp crossing same a little below a foard called
Archibald Thomas foard, thence by John Wallers Shop & into
his field, thence a direct line to Limestone crossing at a
foard called Waggon foard, thence along by Archibald Thomas
fence a direct course until it comes into a path called
Filyaws Road thence near as said path or road runs crossing
Gourd Branch & to the County line; Court concurred.

Appointed Joseph T. Rhodes Overseer of said New Road & have
following hands: Archibald Thomas, William Basden, Samuel
Whaley, William Whaley, Sr., William Whaley, Jr., Job Hunter,
Benjamin Padget, Isaac Padget, William Hunter, Edward Hunter,
Stephen Hancock, Jesse Brown, Matthew Edwards, Joseph T.
Rhodes, Nathan Waller, Isaac Whaley, John Waller, Job Hunter.

Reporte of Committee appointed to inspect Limestone Bridge
Exhibited by Hugh McCanne; Court concurred & Ordered filed.

Bond from Frederick Dowell to Court for Building a Bridge
across NorthEast River at mouth of Limestone Creek, Exhibited; Ordered recorded & filed.

William Basden being Scited to appear before this Court to
show cause why he did not appear as a witness in behalf of
State against Thomas Quinn, make oath he never was noticed;
Ordered he be discharged.

Account rendered by John Fleming, Adm'r of Nathan Boyet, dec'd, amounting to £4-0-9 Exhibited; Court concurred & Ordered recorded.

Account & Settlement made by Edward Pearsall, Guardian to John James Midleton, by which it appears there is remaining in hands of said Edward Pearsall the sum of £415-2-8; Court concurred & Ordered filed.

Ordered Grand & Petit Jury have Tickets for one days service this Term.

Allowed Peleg Rogers & Moses Manning 8 shillings each for one days services as constable.

Thursday Morning [19 Jan 1804]   Court met a 10 o'clock according to adjournment.

Present: Worshipful James Pearsall, Hugh McCanne, James Dickson, Edward Pearsall.

Ordered following be Jurymen next Court: Stephen Miller, Jeremiah Pearsall, Jonathan Thomas, Moses Manning, Benjamin Padget, James Lanier, Jr., Samuel Whaley, Lincoln Shuffield, George Brice, Bryan Farrior, George Houston, James Williams, Caleb Quinn, Christopher Lawson, Alexander Keaton, Willis Hines, Edward Alberson, Samuel Davis, Elisha Herring, Isham Faison, James Ward, Lewis Carleton, David Davis, Abraham Newton, Austin Beesley, Isaac Spence, Jesse Reeves, William Johnston, Jesse Watkins, John Thally, Daniel Murphy, Jacob Wells (I.C.), William Hall, Jr.; Robert Sloan, Theophilus Swinson, David Quinn, Daniel Mallard, John Hunter, Edward Armstrong, And'w McIntire.

Petit Jury who answered this Court are: William Stoakes, Stephen Williams, Benjamin Dulany, Abner Cottle, Benjamin Herring, James Price, Moses Stanley, John Beck, John Byrd, Joseph Dickson, Merrit Manning, Samuel Houston.

Reporte of Committee on allowance for Mary Blackmore for one year Exhibited; Court concurred & Ordered recorded.

Inventory of Estate of Hezekiah Bell, dec'd, Exhibited by Martha Bell; Ordered recorded.

Account of sale of Hezekiah Bell, dec'd, amounting to £9-17-2 exhibited by Martha Bell; Ordered recorded.

Additional return of sale of part of Estate of Lewis Thomas, dec'd, Exhibited by James Reardon; Ordered recorded.

Andrew Gufford suggested there was an error in his Grant for 150 acres in this County dated 12 March 1800 [No.] 1657; Court upon inquiry found no error but the location being wrong, Patent says beginning at a Black Gum in Hookers Marsh & it is proved to Court that said beginning is on Herrings Marsh which is a different Water Course; Ordered Clerk certifie same.

Appointed Thomas Garrison Overseer of Road from middle of Maxwell at Chastens foard to where said Road enters William Fredericks Avenue & have same hands that William Carr had.

Appointed Hogan Hunter Overseer of Road from Fredericks Cross Road to the Court House & have John McGowens hands, Widow McGowens hands & his own hands to work under him.

Allowed William Dickson, Clerk of this Court, £20 for extra services last year, 1803.

Sundry Deeds & Bills of Sale being proved & Acknowledged in Court this Term, Ordered Clerk record them when at his own house.

Court Adjourned Till Court in Course.

[signed] James Dickson, Edw'd Pearsall, Hugh McCanne

Minutes of January Term, 1804, continued. [Day & date not given]

John Hunter, charged with begeting a Bastard Child of Margaret New, gave Bond required by Law.

Appointed William A. Houston, Richard Chasten, John Byrd, Merrit Manning, William Matthis & Timothy Spence constables & they have given Bond.

Bill of Sale: Lewis Davis to James Rhodes for a Negro man Skiff, proved by William Southerland; Ordered registered.

Bill of Sale: Robert McGowen to Andrew McIntire for a Negro boy Sam, proved by William McGowen; Ordered registered.

Bill of Sale: Alexander O'Daniel to Owen O'Daniel for a Negro wench Rach & her two children, Grace & Milley & a Negro wench Fib & sundry other articles, proved by Edward Outlaw; Ordered registered.

Bill of Sale: Stephen Herring to Owen O'Daniel for a Negro wench Fib, proved by William Glisson; Ordered registered.

Bill of Sale: William Dunkan to Henry Bowden for a Negro girl Easter, Acknowledged; Ordered registered.

Bill of Sale: William O'Daniel to Charity O'Daniel for a Negro girl Phib, proved by Owen O'Daniel; Ordered registered.

Bill of Sale: Jonathan Keithly to James Bailey for a Negro girl Easter, Acknowledged; Ordered registered.

Bill of Sale: Jesse Williams to David Quinn for a Negro boy Nathan, Acknowledged; Ordered registered.

Bill of Sale: Stephen King to John Byrd for a Negro man Titus, proved by Thomas Wright; Ordered registered.

Bill of Sale: Thomas Powell to John Byrd for a Negro girl Fibby, proved by David Clark; Ordered registered.

["Deed: James Wright to Isaac Wright for 550 acres, Acknowledged; Ordered registered" marked through.] Withdrawn by Isaac Wright.

Deed: Hardy Parker to Lot Green for 100 acres, proved by Aaron Williams; Ordered registered.

Deed: Theophilus Guy to Anthony Drew for 50 acres, Acknowledged; Ordered registered.

Deed: Adam Platt to William Browning for 100 acres, proved by John Gilman; Ordered registered.

Deed: David Brock to William Southerland for 280 acres, Acknowledged; Ordered registered.

Deed: Hardy Powell to Joseph Stringfield for 400 acres, proved by William Bland; Ordered registered.

Deed: Thomas Green & John Green to Lot Green for 50 acres, proved by Aaron Williams; Ordered registered.

Deed: Henry Cannon to David Clark for 1140 acres, Acknowledged; Ordered registered.

Deed: Stephen Williams to Cloe Williams for 100 acres, proved by Nathan Waller; Ordered registered.

Deed: William Rigby to John Cooper, Jr. for 130 acres, proved by Jonathan Thomas; Ordered registered.

Deed: Joel Hines to Matthew Ward for 100 acres, Acknowledged; Ordered registered.

Deed: Samuel Alberson to Alexander Keaton for 200 acres, proved by Daniel Glisson; Ordered registered.

Deed: John Winders to Moses Stanley for 4 pieces of land, Acknowledged; Ordered registered.

Deed: Stratten Burton to William Pickett, Sr. for 200 acres, proved by Arthur Murray; Ordered registered.

Deed: Thomas Cook to Thomas Wells for two pieces of land, proved by Frederick Wells; Ordered registered.

Deed: Jacob Matthis to Hansel Ezell for 100 acres, proved by Jacob Matthis, Jr.; Ordered registered.

Deed: Bryan Medlin to James Matthews for 100 acres, proved by Edward Alberson; Ordered registered.

Deed: Elijah Tucker to William Gore for 100 acres, proved by William Matthis; Ordered registered.

Deed: Elijah Tucker to William Gore for 125 acres, proved by William Matthis; Ordered registered.

Deed: Alexander Carter to Henry Graddy for 85 acres, proved by Thomas Graddy; Ordered registered.

Deed of Gift: Jonathan Davis to David Davis for sundries, proved by David Williams; Ordered registered.

Deed: Joseph Dickson to John Holden for 600 acres, proved by Alexander Dickson; Ordered registered.

Deed: Hezekiah Duncan, Jane Duncan & Henry Cook to Henry Hulet for 150 acres, proved by Thomas Evens; Ordered registered.

Deed: Benjamin Lanier & Jacob Lanier to John Holden for 100 acres, proved by Jehu Wilkinson; Ordered registered.

Deed: Hugh McCanne, Sheriff to William Picket for 87 1/2 acres, Acknowledged; Ordered registered.

Deed: James Philyaw to James Mashburn, Jr. for 124 acres, proved by Amos Johnston; Ordered registered.

Deed: Peter Watkins to John Mercer for 750 acres, proved by Thomas Price; Ordered registered.

[Day & date not given]

Deed: Nicholas Bowden to Thomas Price for 90 acres, proved by Redden Bowden; Ordered registered.

A Division of land of Edward Blackmore, dec'd, which was laid off to Mary Blackmore, widow of said dec'd, rendered by Committee appointed for that purpose (reported to be 300 acres); Court concurred & Ordered registered.

Court Adjourned Till Court in Course.

[signed] James Dickson, Edward Pearsall, Hugh McCanne.

Tes: Wm. Dickson, C.C.

16 April 1804 County Court begun & held for County of Duplin at the Court House, the third Monday.

Present: Worshipfull James Outlaw, Esq. who adjourned Court.

Tuesday Morning [17 Apr 1804] Court met at ten o'clock according to adjournment.

Present: Worshipful James Kenan, Hugh McCanne, Timothy Teachy, Esquires.

Sarah Mathews prayed for an allowence against Phillip Coley for her lying in Expences when delivered of two children which she charged to said Philip Coley; Ordered said Philip Coley shall pay said Sarah Matthis the sum of £10 for nursing & maintaining said children ten months ending this day & Clerk issue execution for same.

Grand Jury sworn: Stephen Miller, foreman, Edward Armstrong, James Williams, Andrew McIntire, Jacob Wells, David Davis, Moses Manning, William Hall, Jr., John Hunter, George Brice, Jesse Watkins, Lewis Carlton, Isam Faison, Samuel Davis.

Ordered Thomas Evens, Constable, attend Grand Jury.

Granted Adm'n of Estate of Jethro Butler, dec'd, to Thomas Goff who gave Bond of £500 & took Oath of Adm'n, Edward Alberson & John Maxwell as securities; Ordered letters issued etc, pd 16/.

Appointed John Matthis a Constable, he gave Bond according to Law.

Jones Smith prayed an Order to turn the Road a small distance out of its present course to lead it out of his plantation & remove it farther from his Doore, which will not exceed one hundred yards in length more than it is now; Granted, he making the same good at his own expence.

Granted Adm'n of Estate of William Rigby, dec'd, jointly to William Rigby & Owen Rigby who gave Bond £1,000 & took Oath of Adm'r; paid 16/.

Granted Adm'n of Estate of Samuel Ward, dec'd, to Andrew Hurst on the resignation of Mary Ward the Widow of said dec'd, said Andrew Hurst gave Bond of £300 & took Oath of Adm'r.

Granted Adm'n of Estate of Elisha Jernigan, dec'd, to Zilpah Jernigan & Charles Gibbs, they gave Bond of £1500 & took Oath of Adm'r.

Granted Adm'n of Estate of Jacob Mainor, dec'd, to Charity Mainor who gave Bond of £250 & took Oath of Adm'r; pd 16/.

Inventory of Estate of Elisha Jernigan, dec'd, Exhibited by Charles Gibbs; Ordered filed & Recorded.

Ordered Adm'r of Elisha Jernigan, dec'd, sell Estate of said dec'd & reporte to next Court.

Bryan Bowden, Esq., Nicholas Bowden & Leven Watkins are appointed a Committee to lay out to Zilpah, widow of Elisha Jernigan, dec'd, one years provisions for her & her family & make return to next Court.

Deed: Hugh McCanne, Sheriff, to Daniel Glisson for 199 acres, proved by Charles Hooks; Ordered registered.

Appointed Samuel Herring a Constable in this County for one year, he gave Bond.

Ordered Admin'rs of William Rigby, dec'd, sell Perishable Estate of said dec'd & Reporte to next Court.

Edward Pearsall, Esq., James Midleton & David Midleton are appointed a Committee to lay off one years Provisions for Elizabeth Rigby, widow of William Rigby, dec'd, for herself & family & return same to next Court.

Appointed Love Savage a Constable for ensuing year, he gave Bond.

Sale of a Negro Wench Peg of Estate of Ebenezer Garrison for £250-2-0 by Order of Court was Exhibited by John Farrior; Ordered recorded.

Hugh McCanne, Esq., late Sheriff of this County prayed for an allowance for his extra services as Sheriff for 1801 and 1802; Court allowed £30 for 1801 & £30 for 1802; Ordered Clerk certifie same.

Edward Alberson appointed Overseer of the Road in room of Samuel Davis & to have same District & hands.

Ordered also that the Road be moved across from Outlaws lain to meet the same & that David Alberson, Edward Outlaw, Alexander Outlaw & Richard Matthews work under him.

Ordered Edward Alberson, Alexander Outlaw, Samuel Davis, James Matthews, Edward Outlaw, David Alberson, Alexander Keaton, Henry Graddy (buckswamp), Jonathan Keithly, Henry Graddy (Merch't), Frederick Graddy & James Outlaw be a Jury to lay off same & that James Outlaw Qualifie said Jury.

Appointed Jonathan Brooks Overseer of the River in stead of Daniel Murray & have same District & hands to wit: Daniel Murray, James Cavenagh, David Sloan, William Johnston, William Hanchy, William Cavenagh, William Picketts Negro Sam & Arthur Murrays Sam & Dan'l Murrays Ben.

Appointed William Boney Overseer of the Road in room of John Williams & have same District & hands.

Appointed James Reardon Guardian to Sally Thomas, Rebecka Thomas & Sena Thomas, Orphans of Lewis Thomas: he gave Bond of £10,000; Ordered he take their Estates into his Possession, etc.

In suit of Jonathan Fryer vs. David Cannon & Adm'rs of Edward Blackmore, Jury empannelled & find in hands of Adm'rs of Edward Blackmore the sum of £90 due Plaintiff from said Adm'rs as Garnishees execution not to issue by Default & Enquirey as to David Cannon & the Jury assess the Plaintiffs Damage to £150; On motion the above sum of £90 condemned in hands of said Garnishees; Appeal prayed & Granted, Bond given by William Hill.

Reporte of Committee appointed to settle accounts of Estate of Barbara Murphy with Frederick Wells, Ex'r, was Exhibited

by which it appears there remains in hands of Frederick Wells
a ballance of 42-5-10; Court concurred & Ordered recorded.

Ordered Hezekiah Millard & Micajah Cannon be ad[d]ed to District of Road where Jesse Swinson is Overseer & that they &
their hands shall work under said Jesse Swinson.

Byrd Williams, Thomas Wells, John Maxwell & Peter Carleton
having served as Patrollers last year are allowed 40/ each.

John Gilman is appointed Overseer of the Road in room of
James Harrell & is to have same District & hands.

A Reporte of the Division of the Estate of Peter Young,
dec'd, Exhibited; Court concurred & Ordered recorded.

Pursuant to Petition of Sundry Persons praying for a New Road
to be laid off from the Old Road at Thomas Heaths & leading
down on the South side of Maxwell by Robert Sloans Cart Road
to join the Island Creek Road near the Meeting House which is
Granted.

Ordered Theophilus Swinson, David Quinn, Thomas Heath, William Matchet, Amos Shuffield, James Dickson, Nicholas Bryan,
John Maxwell, John Thally, John Chambers, John Linton, Gideon
Arthur, Samuel Chambers & Jacob Wells be a Jury to view & lay
off said new Road & Reporte to next Court. And that Gibson
Sloan, Esq. Qualifie said Jury & Peleg Rogers, Constable
convene said Jury.

Reporte of Committee appointed to settle accounts of Estate
of Amos Johnston with Nathan Waller & Arthur Murray the Ex'rs
was exhibited by which it appears there remains in hands of
Ex'rs the ballance of £107-16-1; Court concurred & Ordered
recorded.

Michael Boney Petitioned for his Negro fellow [name left
blank] to carry a gun on his own Plantation for defence of
his Stock, etc.; Granted with said Michael Boney complying
with Terms of Law in such case made & provided, Ordered Clerk
take Bond.

Charles Hooks, Samuel Dunn & James Clark are appointed a
Committee to divide Estate of Lewis Thomas, dec'd, among the
Heirs agreeable to Will & Reporte to next Court.

James Kenan, Esq., Andrew McIntire & Andrew Hurst are ap-
pointed a Committee to settle the accounts of Estate of John
Johnston, dec'd, with James Wright & Edward Pearsall, Adm'rs
& Reporte to this Court.

<u>Wednesday Morning [18 Apr 1804]</u> Court met at ten o'clock
according to adjournment.

Present: Worshipfull James Kenan, Joseph T. Rhodes, William
Beck, Daniel Glisson, James Maxwell, Hugh McCanne & Charles
Hooks, Esquires.

Last Will & Testament of Stephen Rogers Exhibited & proved by
Edward Armstrong & Ancrum Averit the subscribing witnesses &
at same time John Hunter & Thomas McGee, two of Executors
named in said Will, Qualified.

Report of Committee appointed to settle accounts of Estate of
Ebenezer Garrison dec'd, with John Farrior, Adm'r, Exhibited
by which it appears there is a ballance of £301-18-4 out of
which sum James Garrison is Intituled to £75-9-7, being the
fourth part & his distributive share; Ordered same recorded.

Reporte of the Committee appointed to lay off the Dower of
land of John Balcom dec'd, to Hester Balcom, widow of said
dec'd, is as follows: Beginning at a pine the Original Corner running thence as the old line S 57 E 188 pole to a pine,
the other old corner thence N 60 E 156 to a pine, thence N 57
W 188 pole to a stake in the field, thence to the beginning
which includes the Dwelling House & most of the Improvements
of said dec'd; Court concurred & Ordered recorded.

Proceeding of an Inquisition held on the body of Hicks Mills,
dec'd, held on the 21 Nov. 1803 was rendered by Robert Southerland, Esq., Corroner of this County which states that the
said Hicks Mills came by his death by an accident occasioned
by a bruise in his bowells, without any Premeditated inten-
tion or malice aforethought of any Person; Ordered said
Inquisition recorded.

Inventory of Estate of Samuel Ward, dec'd, Exhibited by
Andrew Hurst; Ordered recorded.

Ordered Andrew Hurst, Adm'r of Samuel Ward, dec'd, sell the
Estate of said dec'd & Reporte same to next Court.

William Beck, Esq., Samuel Dunn & David Wright are appointed
a Committee to lay off to Mary Ward, widow of Samuel Ward,
dec'd, one years provisions of her dec'd husbands Estate &
reporte to next Court.

["Reporte of settlement of accounts of Estate of John Johnston, dec'd. with James Wright & Edward Pearsall, Adm'rs was
rendered by Committee appointed, which states that the accounts of said Adm'rs are correct" marked through.]

Ordered a Tax of four pence on each & every Poll Taxable & of
one Penney on each & every 100 acres of land in this County
be levied & Collected by the Sheriff for purpose of building
a bridge over Rockfish Creek.

Appointed William Stokes, Jr. Guardian to Anna Murphy, Elisabeth Murphy, Easther Murphy & Henry Murphy, Children of William Murphy, he gave Bond of £2,000; Ordered he take Estates
of said four children into his possession.

Ordered Ex'rs of Timothy Murphy, dec'd, upon application of
William Stoakes, Guardian to Anna, Elisabeth, Easther & Henry
Murphy, Children of William Murphy do deliver to said William
Stoakes all papers, Notes, bonds, Monies & Property of Estate
of said Timothy Murphy now belonging to said Children of
William Murphy which is in their possession & take his reciet
for same.

Appointed John Maxwell Guardian to Nancy Carr, Minor Orphan,
he gave Bond of £3,000; Ordered he take her Estate into his
possession.

Edward Pearsall, James Maxwell & Jehu Wilkinson are appointed
a Committee to divide the Estate of James Carr, dec'd, among
the Orphans of said dec'd, agreeable to his Will & Reporte to
next Court.

Appointed Leven Watkins Guardian to Lewis Thomas, Minor Orphan of Lewis Thomas, dec'd, he gave Bond of £4,000; Ordered
he take his Estate into his possession.

William Dickson, Clerk of this Court, purchased two large
bound books for the Records of the Court which cost him $7.50
which he paid: Ordered Sheriff do pay the said William Dickson the said $7.50 out of the County Tax & that he be allowed
same in setling his accounts with the Court.

An Additional account of the Sale of the Estate of Edward
Blackmore, dec'd, was rendered by William Hill, Adm'r; Ordered recorded.

Hogan Hunter appointed Overseer of the Road from the Court
House to the Middle of Persimmon Swamp & to have same hands
he formerly had.

James Raphel appointed Overseer of the River in room of John
Murrow from Rogers old landing down to limestone Bridge &
have the following hands: two from And'w McIntire, two from
James Gillespie, one from William McGowen, two from Robert
Twilley and two from John T. Rhodes.

George Houston appointed Overseer of the River from Soracta
to Rogers landing & have following hands to work under him:
John Neale & his Negroes Mingo, London & Dick; William
Houston, Geo. Williamses Negroes Kitt & Jim.

Last Will & Testament of John Knowles Exhibited & proved by
Amos Tucker, one of subscribing witnesses & at same time
David Carleton, one of the Executors named in said Will,
Qualified; pd. 16/.

Ordered Henry Houston, Minor, bound Apprentice to John Wilkinson till age 21 to learn to Read the Bible & Arithmetic as
far as the Rule of Three.

Appointed Peleg Rogers a Constable, he gave bond.

Allowed Love Savage 16/ for attending Court two days as Constable this Term.

Allowed Thomas Evens 16/ for attending Court as Constable two
days this Term.

An additional Sale of Estate of Thomas Norment, dec'd,
amounting to £199-5-0 was Exhibited by David Wright, one of
the Ex'rs; Ordered recorded.

Committee appointed to lay off to the Widow of Benajah Mobley, dec'd, one years Provisions to the 8th day of March
next, have allowed her five hogs, one Beef & $6 to purchase
Corn; Court concurred & Ordered recorded.

Following appointed Jurymen to Wilmington Superior Court on
the 13 May next: Joseph T. Rhodes, Charles Hooks, William
Southerland, Joseph Dickson, Bazil Kornegay, Gibson Sloan,
William Pickett.

Reports of Committee appointed to settle accounts of Estate
of John Johnston, dec'd, with James Wright & Edward Pearsall,
Adm'rs, was rendered which states that accounts of said
Adm'rs are correct & the said Committee state that there is
due the said Adm'rs for sundry expences the sum of £53; Court
concurred & Ordered County Wardens pay same to said James
Wright & Edward Pearsall out of Parish Tax & Exclusive of the
Monies of the Estate of said John Johnston deposited in their
hands.

As an Order of the Court was passed authorizing the Sheriff
to Convene a Jury to try the Property of a certain Tract of
land the Property of Jerediah Bass Foley & claimed by Stephen
Jones, on which land sundry Executions have been levied on

Judgements against said Jerediah Bass Foley, the said Jury
when convened have decreed that the claim of Stephen Jones is
fraudulent, etc; Ordered Sheriff sell the land to satisfie
the said Executions levied thereon.

Reports of Committee appointed to divide the Lands & Negroes
of David Peale, dec'd, among the several Heirs have made
return of said Division: Court concurred & Ordered Recorded
as follows:
There is 430 acres to be divided among four claimants-
To Bryan Minshew and wife who drew the 4th Lott, containing
102 acres, including Houses & part of the Plantation at
£100-0-0;
To John Peale who drew the 3rd Lott containing 112 acres,
including a part of the field at £75-0-0;
To William Peale, a Minor, Grandson of said David Peal,
dec'd, and also an Heir who drew the 2nd Lott containing 107
acres at £40-2-6;
To Robert Peale, who drew the first Lott containing 109 acres
at £40-2-6;
The division of the Negroes were as follows:
To William Peale who had a Deed of Gift from his father David
Peale, dec'd, for a Negro girl Winney, valued at £170;
To Robert Peale who drew a Negro boy Ben at £167-5-0;
To Bryan Minshew & wife who drew an old Negro man named Bazoo
at £35-0-0;
To John Peale who drew a Negro woman Easter at £175-0-0;
Court concurred & Ordered recorded.

An Instrument in writing from Daniel Glisson to Stephen
Bright Herring, Ex'r of Stephen Herring, dec'd, was presented
& proved by David Midleton & admitted to be Recorded in following words:
Pursuant to a Clause in the Last Will & Testament of Stephen
Herring late of Duplin Co, dec'd, Relating to me & my Children by my wife Sally Glisson, Daughter of said Stephen Herring, I have received from Stephen Bright Herring, one of
Ex'rs of said Will of Stephen Herring, the two Negro girls
directed in said Will to be purchased by said Stephen Bright
Herring & delivered to me for the use of my Children by the
said Sally Glisson my former wife - For which I do hereby
acknowledge that as the father of the said Children I have
received their said legacies, the said two Negro girls in
full from the said Stephen B. Herring for the use of my said
Children for which I do hereby Acquit & discharge the said
Stephen Bright Herring from all claims or demands of me or of
any of the Children of my said former wife Sally Glisson for
any legacies or Portions etc. due from said Estate to me or
any of the said Children agreeable to the words & true intent
and meaning of the said last Will & Testament respecting me &
my said Children & I do hereby indemnifie & save harmless the

said Stephen B. Herring from all Claims, damages & costs which may arise to the said Stephen B. Herring in consequence of the delivery of the said two Negro girls to me, or by reason of any other matter or thing relative to the Premises. In Witness whereof, I the said Daniel Glisson have hereunto set my hand & Seal this 17th day of April 1804. D. Glisson Witness: David Midleton.

Bill of Sale: Bryan Edmonson to Francis Oliver for a Negro boy Willie, proved by Jo. Dickson; Ordered registered.

Bill of Sale: Stephen Herring to William Brown for a Negro woman Jane, proved by Aaron Williams; Ordered registered.

Bill of Sale: Dennis Cannon to Abraham Cannon for a Negro Frank, proved by William Pollock; Ordered registered.

Bill of Sale: John Gibbs, Sr. to Henry Bowden for a Negro boy Simon, proved by Charles Gibbs; Ordered registered.

Bill of Sale: Stephen B. Herring to William Branch for a Negro boy Dave, Acknowledged; Ordered registered.

Bill of Sale: William Johnston [no Grantee] for a Negro man James, proved by Elisha Williford; Ordered registered.

Deed of Gift: Edward Houston & Mary Houston to their daughter Rebecka Houston for a Negro boy Limbrick, proved by Jacob Williams; Ordered registered.

Deed: Thomas Sheppard to Samuel Midleton for 109 acres, Acknowledged; Ordered registered.

Deed: William Cavanagh to James Cavanagh for 180 acres, proved by Daniel Murray; Ordered registered.

Deed: Isaac Spence to John Kornegay for 40 acres, Acknowledged; Ordered registered.

Deed: Samuel Herring to William Whitfield for 171 acres, Acknowledged; Ordered registered.

Deed: John Winders, Jr. to John Winders, Sr. for 355 acres, proved by Edward Winders; Ordered registered.

Deed: Jonathan Keithly to Lewis Herring for 350 acres, proved by James Outlaw; Ordered registered.

Deed: Thomas E. James to William Hall, Sr. for 372 acres, proved by Thomas McGee; Ordered registered.

Deed: Abraham Newton to James Newton for 173 acres,
Acknowledged; Ordered registered.

Deed: Nehemiah Forehand to Lewis Herring for 135 acres,
proved by James Outlaw; Ordered registered.

Deed: Michael Wilkings to William Whitfield for 25 acres,
proved by Samuel Herring; Ordered registered.

Deed: Jesse Reaves to Jesse Norris for 40 acres, proved by
William Taylor; Ordered registered.

Deed: Zachariah Harris to Samuel Herring for 80 acres,
proved by Hardy Reeves; Ordered registered.

Deed: Hardy Reeves to Samuel Herring for 91 acres, Acknowledged; Ordered registered.

Deed: Uriah Harris to George Hays for 100 acres, proved by
Samuel Herring; Ordered registered.

Deed: Mordicai Mobley to William Pickett for 87 1/2 acres,
proved by William Johnston; Ordered registered.

Deed: William Hall, Sr. to Thomas Sheppard for four parcels
land, containing 372 acres, Acknowledged; Ordered registered.

Deed: William Harris to Samuel Herring for 200 acres, proved
by Hardy Reeves; Ordered registered.

Deed: Jesse Norris to Jesse Reeves for 40 acres, proved by
William Taylor; Ordered registered.

Deed: Robert Wallace to William James for 300 acres, proved
by Aaron Williams; Ordered registered.

Deed: William James to Robert Wallace for 220 acres, proved
by Aaron Williams; Ordered registered.

Deed: Thomas Findley to Benjamin Cooper for 325 acres,
proved by William Beck, Jr.; Ordered registered.

Deed: John Sulliven to Stephen Herring for 25 acres, proved
by Lewis Sullivent; Ordered registered.

Deed: William Alberson to Samuel Alberson for 2 pieces land
of 275 acres, proved by Thomas Wright; Ordered registered.

Deed: Michael Glisson to Jonathan Keithly for 48 acres,
Acknowledged; Ordered registered.

Deed: Whitfield Herring to Stephen Herring for 50 acres,
proved by Owen O'Daniel; Ordered registered.

Deed: George Memory to Peter Foreman Price for 2 pieces land
of 110 acres, proved by Bazil Kornegay; Ordered registered.

Deed: Benjamin Snipes to Stephen Herring for 15 acres,
proved by Bryan Glisson; Ordered registered.

Deed: Major Searles to Bryan Whitfield for 2 pieces land,
130 acres, Acknowledged; Ordered registered.

Deed: Benjamin Ellis to James Houston for 11 lotts in
Soracta Town, proved by John Houston; Ordered registered.

Deed: John Wilkinson to Ben Johnston for 200 acres, Acknowledged; Ordered registered.

Deed: Samuel Alberson to Jesse Branch for ["25 acres" marked
through] sundry pieces of land, proved by Loftis Worley;
Ordered registered.

Appointed William Hudgeons constable for one year in this
County; he gave Bond.

Joseph T. Rhodes, William Southerland & John Farrior are
appointed a Committee to divide the Personal Estate of Amos
Johnston, dec'd, amongst the several Claimants agreeable to
the Will & Reporte to next Court.

Petit Jury allowed Tickets for services for two days each
this Term: Jeremiah Pearsall, Benjamin Padget, George
Houston, Abraham Newton, Isaac Spence, John Thally, Daniel
Murphy, Robert Sloan, Theophilus Swinson, Daniel Mallard.

Ordered Grand Jury have Tickets for 2 days also.

Appointed following Justices take lists of Taxables in this
County this year:
    For Capt. Manings Co. - Ben Lanier, Esq.
    For Capt. Browns Co. - Rob't Southerland, Esq.
    For Capt. Houstons Co. - Jacob Williams, Esq.
    For Capt. Pearsalls Co. - Edw'd Pearsall, Esq.
    For Capt. J. A. Swinsons Co. - Dan'l Glisson, Esq.
    For Capt. Jesse Swinsons Co. - Sampson Grimes, Esq.
    For Capt. Millards Co. - William Duncan, Esq.
    For Capt. Herrings Co. - Charles Hooks, Esq.
    For Capt. Willis Co. - Gibson Sloan, Esq.
    For Capt. D. Williams Co. - D'd Williams, Esq.
    For Capt. Carrs Co. - Hugh McCanne, Esq.
    For Capt. Midletons Co. - James Dickson, Esq.

Ordered following be Jurymen to next Court: Jonathan Thomas,
James Chambers, Joseph Grimes, William Johnston, Nathan Foun-
tain, Samuel Whaley, Lincoln Shuffield, Lewis Davis, Bryan
Farrior, Caleb Quin, Richard Swinson, Samuel Houston, Willis
Hines, David King, Alex'r Keaton, Sam'l Davis, Edward Alber-
son, James Ward, Elias Faison, Benjamin Hodges, Thomas Kenan,
Aaron Williams, William Swetman, William Stoakes, William
Johnston, John Beck, Hezekiah Millard, John Kornegay, Nat.
McCanne, John McCanne, John Gilman, Lewis Chambers, William
Higgins, Alexander Dickson, Abraham Hall, Benjamin Brown,
John Murray, Jehu Wilkinson.

Moses Mannin & Benjamin Padget having served as Patrollers in
1803 are allowed 40 shillings each.

Account of Sale of part of Estate of John Williams, dec'd,
which was laid off for Edward Williams amounting to £36-16-6
was Exhibited by Temperence Williams, Guardian to said Edward
Williams; Ordered recorded.

Court Adjourned Till Court in Course.

[signed] Jas Kenan, Jas Maxwell, William Southerland, Edw'd
Pearsall.

16 July 1804 County Court Begun & held for County of Duplin at
the Court House, the 3rd Monday.

Present: Worshipfull Edward Pearsall, Esq. who adjourned
Court.

Tuesday Morning [17 Jul 1804] Court met at 9 o'clock according
to adjournment.

Present: Worshipfull James Kenan, Daniel Glisson, Edward
Pearsall, William Duncan, James Maxwell, Esquires.

Grand Jury sworn: Jehu Wilkinson, foreman, Hezekiah Millard,
Ben Hodges, William Johnston, William Swetman, Richard Swin-
son, Nathan Fountain, Jonathan Thomas, John Gilman, Caleb
Quin, John Kornegay, Nath'l McCanne, Sam'l Davis.

David Durell appointed Overseer of the Road in room of Moses
Stanley & have same District & hands.

Petit Jury Qualified: Aaron Williams, Joseph Grimes, John
Murrow, Benjamin Brown, William Higgins, Lewis Chambers, John
McCanne, William Stoakes, Edward Alberson, Samuel Houston,
Lewis Davis - 1 day - , James Chambers.

Ordered Thomas Johnston, Dawson Turner & all hands in the
family of William Brock shall work on the Newbern Road under
John Thigpen, Overseer.

Moses Stanley petitioned for leave to turn the Road through
his Plantation about a quarter of a mile which will not add
any to the length of said Road & which he will repair at his
own expence; Granted.

Ordered Merrit Maning, Constable, attend Grand Jury.

Ordered Adm'x of Jacob Mainor, dec'd, sell Estate of said
dec'd & return same to next Court.

Elizabeth Rigby is appointed Guardian to Bryant Rigby,
Russell Rigby, Kitty Rigby, Beckey & Sally Rigby, the five
children of William Rigby, dec'd, she gave Bond of £2,000;
Ordered she take their Estates into Possession.   pd 6/.

["James Pearsall, James Midleton, Sr. & David Midleton are
appointed a Committee to divide Estate of William Rigby,
dec'd between the Widow & five children & Reporte to next
Court" marked through.]

Henry Bowden is appointed Guardian to Sally Jernigan, a Minor
Orphan, he gave Bond of £500; Ordered he take her Estate
into his possession.

Samuel Bowden is appointed Guardian to John Jernigan, Minor
Orphan, he gave Bond of £500; Ordered he take his Estate
into his possession.

Nathan Fountain recorded his mark, an under square in each
ear.

Court proceeded to Elect a Sheriff & unanimously Elected
James Hall, Esq. to that office for the ensuing year;
Ordered Clerk certifie same that Commission may issue.

William Guy, Sr. appointed Overseer of the Road in room of
Isaac Wright & to have same District & hands.

Granted William McCanne Adm'n of Estate of Abigal Parker, he
gave Bond of £100 & took Oath of Adm'r.

Ordered Adm'r of Abigal Parker, dec'd, sell Estate of said
dec'd & make return to next Court.

Peter Frederick, Isam Faison, Felix K. Hill, Alfred Beck are
appointed Patrollers for up[p]er end of Capt. Herrings Co.

John Cooper, Jr. prayed for an Order to Build a Public Grist
Mill on the run of Grove Swamp where he is the owner of the
land on one side & the Heirs of William Rigby are owners on
the other side, The Guardian of said Orphans of said William
Rigby being present & Consenting; Granted.

Jeremiah Pearsall, Benjamin Best & John Best are appointed a
Committee to lay off & value one, or as much as they may deem
sufficiant, acre of land of the Estate of William Rigby,
dec'd, for the purpose of building a Public Grist Mill which
is Granted to John Cooper, Jr. & make return to next Court.

James Pearsall, Edward Pearsall & John Johnston are appointed
a Committee to make a final settlement of Estate of James
Chambers, dec'd, with Jeremiah Pearsall the Adm'r & to ascer-
tain what part of said Estate yet due & coming to James &
Abraham, two of the Claimants thereof & make return to next
Court.

Samuel Davis, being bro't before the Court & charged with begeting a Bastard Child of Sarah Winfield, gave Bond required
by law.

Ordered John Heath be exempted from paying a Poll Tax or
working on the Roads.

Job Hunter, John Padget & Matthew Sumner having served as
patrollers last year are allowed each 30/.

Aaron Williams, John Williams, John Huffham & Abraham Newton
appointed Patrollers in District of Capt. David Williams Co.

Jacob Monk, Jacob Matthis, William Brown & Hardy Carleton
appointed Patrollers in District of Capt. Wells Co.

On Petition of James Armstrong Ordered John McCanne, Daniel
Murphy, William McCanne, William Cook, Richard Chasten,
Nathaniel McCanne, Lincoln Shuffield, James Wallace, James
Pickett, John Gilman, James Harrell & Henry Allen be a Jury
to view & turn the Road from James Armstrongs fence to a
Swamp by the name of Reedy Meadow & that Richard Chasten,
Constable, summon & convene said Jury upon the Premises &
wait on said Jury & that James Armstrong Repair same at his
own expence.

Ordered William Hollingsworth, William Cook, William Pickett,
James Pickett, Sr., Jacob Parker, John Pickett, Lincoln Shuffield, Nathan Fountain, James Lanier, Jr., John Lanier,
William Johnston & Hosea Lanier appointed a Jury to view &
lay off a Road at or near the Plantation of James Williams &
that Merrit Maning, Constable convene & William Southerland,
Esq. Qualifie same.

Ordered Archelaus Branch be Overseer of the Road in room of
Thomas Williams & have same district & hands.

John Southerland is appointed Constable in room of John Byrd,
Resigned; Ordered he give Bond & Qualifie.

Isam Faison is appointed Overseer of the Road in room of
Samuel Dunn & have same District & hands.

Benjamin Bowden is appointed Overseer of the Road in room of
Jesse Swinson & have same District & hands.

Pursuant to an Order of last Court a Jury was convened &
Qualified to lay off a New Road on the South side of Maxwell
leading from the Road at Thomas Heaths to the Wilmington Road
at the Meeting house above Island Creek; Reporte that they
have viewed & laid off said Road nearly as the Cart Road
leads from the head of Thomas Heaths lain Crossing the Beverdam branch & from thence near Theophilus Swinsons lane & from
thence near David Quins New House & from thence to Sloans
bridge on the Beverdam at Sloans field, thence nearly with
said Cart path to the Ridge path near Nicholas Bryans, thence
nearly with a line of marked trees near said Bryans house,
thence as marked by said Jury crossing Mirey[?] branch & by
the head of Wilsons Meadow branch & thence nearly with the
Cart path to where it joins the Road near the Meeting House.

Court concurred & Ordered Amos Shuffield be Overseer of said
New Road & that Theophilus Swinson, David Quin, Jonathan
Hulet, Robert Sloan, Gideon Arthur, John Shuffield, Joseph
Brooks, William Matchet, John Thally, John Bryan, Jacob
Bryan, John Chambers, Samuel Chambers, William Shuffield, &
Chambers's Marcus shall work under him.

Wednesday Morning [18 Jul 1804] Court met at 9 o'clock
according to adjournment.

Present: Worshipfull James Outlaw, William Beck, William
Duncan, James Wright, Charles Hooks, Shadrack Stallings,
William Southerland, Esquires.

Last Will & Testament of Jesse Ellison, dec'd, Exhibited & proved by Isaac Kornegay, one of subscribing witnesses; Ordered filed.

Inventory of Estate of Jacob Mainor, dec'd, Exhibited by Charity Mainor, Am'x; Ordered recorded.

Inventory of Estate of William Rigby, dec'd, Exhibited by William Rigby & Owen Rigby, Adm'rs; Ordered recorded.

Inventory of Estate of Abigal Parker, dec'd, Exhibited by William McCanne, Adm'r; Ordered recorded.

Reports of Settlement of Estate of Henry Maxwell, dec'd, in favour of James Maxwell, a Minor & Claimant, Exhibited; Ordered recorded.

Report of Committee in favour of Zilpah Jernigan, widow of Elisha Jernigan for one years provisions; Court concurred & Ordered recorded.

Reporte of Committee in favour of Mary Ward, Widow of Samuel Ward, dec'd, laying off one years provisions; Court concurred & Ordered recorded.

Reporte of division of Estate of Amos Johnston, dec'd, Exhibited; Court concurred & Ordered recorded.

Account of Sale of Estate of Elisha Jernigan, dec'd, amounting to £259-18-10 Exhibited by Adm'rs; Ordered recorded.

Account of Sales of Estate of Samuel Ward, dec'd, Exhibited; Ordered recorded.

Account of Sale of Estate of William Rigby, dec'd, amounting to £416-11-0 Exhibited by Adm'rs; Ordered recorded.

Reporte of Committee on a Settlement of Estate of Lewis Thomas, dec'd Exhibited by which it appears there is a ballance in hands of Ex'rs amounting to £2948-11-1; Court concurred & Ordered recorded.

Bill of Sale: John Hufham to Aaron Williams for a Negro boy George, proved by Abraham Newton; Ordered Registered.

Bill of Sale: John Byrd to David Wright for a Negro man Titus, Acknowledged; Ordered registered.

Deed: Martin Hanchy to Isam Norris for 100 acres, proved by Reuben Norris; Ordered registered.

Deed: John Carleton to Stephen Herring for 150 acres, proved by Thomas Lanier; Ordered registered.

Deed: Stephen Herring to John Sloan for 100 acres, Acknowledged; Ordered registered.

Deed: James Murray, Sr & Sarah Murray, his wife, to John Murphy for 130 acres, proved by Martin Hanchy; Ordered registered.

Deed: Needham Garner, Sr to Needham Garner for 125 acres, proved by William Garner; Ordered registered.

Deed: James Lanier to William Johnston for 100 acres, Acknowledged; Ordered registered.

Deed: David Brock to Sam'l Sanderlin for 175 acres, proved by Bryan Farrior; Ordered registered.

Deed: Hugh McCanne, Sheriff to William Pickett for 435 acres, Acknowledged; Ordered registered.

Deed: Hugh McCanne, Sheriff to William Pickett for 90 acres, Acknowledged; Ordered registered.

Deed: John Byrd to Michael Byrd for 150 acres, proved by Daniel Kenan; Ordered registered.

Deed: Timothy Murphy to Thomas Lanier for 100 acres, proved by William Stoakes; Ordered registered.

Deed: John Byrd to Maurice Moore for 25 acres, proved by Charles Hooks; Ordered registered.

Deed: David Brock to Henry Southerland for 60 acres, Acknowledged; Ordered registered.

Deed: Job Thigpen to Moses Manning & Nathan Waller for a Meeting House Lott, proved by John Farrior; Ordered registered.

Deed: Fountain Williams to Manuel Carter for 85 acres, proved by Constance Carter; Ordered registered.

Deed: Charles Ward to Stephen Miller for three pieces of land, 290 acres, proved by James Pearsall; Ordered registered.

Deed: Charles Ward to Stephen Miller for certain Priviledges on Land, etc., proved by James Pearsall; Ordered registered.

Deed: Samuel Alberson to Edward Alberson for 200 acres, proved by Edward Winders; Ordered registered.

Deed: Orson Bell to Richard Wolfe for 90 acres, proved by Alexander McMillan; Ordered registered.

Deed: Alexander Carter to Bryan Medlin for 100 acres, proved by Henry Graddy; Ordered registered.

Deed: James Matthews to Edward Alberson for 3 acres, proved by Henry Graddy; Ordered registered.

Deed: Snowden Pearse to Daniel Rainer for 35 acres, proved by Moses Maning; Ordered registered.

Deed: Baker Bowden to Charles Morris for 225 acres, proved by Willie Garner; Ordered registered.

Deed of Gift: Deborah Bell to Martha Bell for a time of Sundry Negroes Services, etc., proved by Abraham Newton; Ordered registered.

Bill of Sale: Jacob Williams to William Hall for a Negro boy Morris, Acknowledged; Ordered registered.

Robert Southerland, Ranger & Stray Master in Duplin Co., made Return of Sundry Strays entered on the Stray book upwards of twelve months past:

    A Stear valued at $10
        Entered by Dennis Cannon
    A two year old Barrow valued at   2.50
        Entered by Merrit Manning
    A Stear valued at   9.
        Entered by John A. Swinson
    A year old Heifer valued at   3.
        Entered by Jacob Brown, Jr.
Ordered Clerk give a list of the above Returns to the County Trustee.

Henry Graddy, being charged with begeting a Bastard Child of Elizabeth Croom, gave Bond required by law.

Martin Kornegay continued Overseer of Road as formerly.

Ordered Luke Kornegay & his two hands be ad[d]ed to Martin Kornegays District of Road & work under him.

William Dickson is continued Overseer of the Road at Goshen Bridge as formerly.

Benjamin Hodges is Continued Overseer of the Road as formerly.

David Hooks is Continued Overseer of the Road as formerly.

Phill Southerland is appointed a Constable, he gave Bond.

Reporte of Committee on the Division of Estate of James Carr, dec'd, Exhibited; Court concurred & Ordered recorded.

["Timothy Teachey" marked out] Jacob Williams, Esq. & Andrew McIntire are appointed inspecters of the Poll in taking & holding the Federal Election in this County the ensuing Election; Ordered Clerk issue Notice thereof.

William Duncan, Esq., Bazil Kornegay are appointed Inspectors of the Poll in the Ensueing Election to be held at Moses Stanleys in this County.

Samuel Houston & Bryan Farrior are appointed Inspectors of the Ensuing Election to be held at the House of Auston Bryan in this County.

Aaron Williams & John Maxwell are appointed Inspectors of the Ensuing Election to be held at the House of David Williams in this County.

Jehu Wilkinson & Joseph Gillespie are appointed Inspectors of the Ensuing Election to be held at the Court House in this County.

George E. Houston, having served as a Patroller for 1797, is allowed 40/ for his services.

George E. Houston, having served as a Patroller in this County for 1802, is allowed 40/ for said services.

John Felix Rhodes having served as a Patroller in this County for 1802 is allowed 40/ for said services.

Deed of Gift: James Dickson, Sr. to his son William Dickson for a Negro boy Amery, Acknowledged; Ordered registered.

Inventory of Estate of John Knowles, dec'd, Exhibited by David Carleton, Ex'r; Ordered recorded.

Deed: Joseph Green to Edward Alberson for 100 acres, proved by William Alberson; Ordered registered.

Daniel Glisson, Hugh McCanne & Thomas Wright, Esquires are appointed Inspecters of Money agreeable to Act of Assembly in 1780, Chap. 12 (Sec Iredell).

Ordered Andrew Stoakes & Luke Huggins be taken from District of Road where Absalom Best is Overseer & ad[d]ed to Benjamin Coopers District & work under him.

John Linton, having served as Patroller in this County in 1795 & also 1799 is allowed 40/ for each year for said services.

Hugh McCanne, William Pickett, Sr. & Auston Bryan appointed a Committee to adjust & settle accounts of Estate of John Lanier, dec'd, with Ex'r & Heirs & Reporte to next Court.

Ordered James Pearsall & Edward Pearsall, Esquires take the Private examination of Mrs. Mary Houston with respect to a certain Deed made by the said Mary & Edward Houston to Stephen Miller for a parcel of land & certifie the same upon the Deed.

Ordered a New Road be laid off from the old Road at Laniers path below his Swamp to the lake ford of Cypress Creek and thence on to the old Wilmington Road at or near the three Mile Meadow & that James Lanier, Sr., John Halso, Hosea Lanier, Nathan Scarborough, Jesse Lanier, Stephen Lanier, Snowdon Pearse, Darling Daffin, Alex'r Mereda[?], Thomas Shoalar, Solomon Shoalar & Levi Shoalar be a Jury to view & lay off said new Road & that Merrit Maning, Constable, summon & convene said Jury on the Premises & Benjamin Lanier, Esq. Qualifie said Jury, & that the Constable return their Proceeding to next Court.

William Williams is appointed Overseer of the Road in room of Howell Best & have same District & hands.

Deed: Richard Normant & Wife to Lewis Chambers for 450 acres, proved by James Hall; Ordered registered.

Merrit Maning is allowed 16/ for attending Court as Constable two days this Term.

Ordered Grand Jury have Certificates for one day this Term.

And the Petit Jury for two days this Term except Lewis Davis who served but one.

Following appointed Jurymen to next Court: David Carleton, John Stallings, Stephen Williams, John Hufham, Daniel Murphy, John Carr, Jesse Lanier, Thomas Coles, James Newton, Felix K. Hill, Daniel Kenan, Elias Faison, Robert Bishop, Henry New- kirk, Benj'n Dulany, Jr., Isaac Midleton, David Midleton, William McGee, Thomas Sheppard, William McGowen, John Hunter, William Bush, Thomas Heath, Benjamin Best, John Cooper, Jr., Chris'r Lawson, Caleb Quin, Henry Graddy, John A. Swinson, William Kornegay, Jr., Stephen Herring (Mill), Stephen Jones, Jesse Swinson, John Beck, William Johnston & John Watkins.

Adm'n of Estate of George Quin Granted to Jacob Williams, Esq., he gave Bond of £100 & took Oath of Adm'r.

Inventory of Estate of George Quin, dec'd Exhibited by Jacob Williams, Adm'r; Ordered recorded. pd. 10/.

Ordered Adm'r of Estate of George Quin, dec'd, sell so much of said Estate sufficient to pay debts & Remainder of said Estate to remain unsold for the support of the Widow & children of said dec'd.

Joseph T. Rhodes, Hugh McCanne, & Edward Pearsall, Esquires, appointed a Committee to settle accounts of Estate of John Brown, dec'd, with Moses Maning, Ex'r & Reporte to next Court.

Joseph T. Rhodes, Hugh McCanne & Edward Pearsall, Esquires are appointed a Committee to settle the accounts of Jesse Lanier, dec'd, with Moses Maning & Hosea Lanier, Admin'rs & return same to next Court.

Joseph T. Rhodes, Hugh McCanne & Edward Pearsall, Esquires are appointed a Committee to settle accounts of Estate of Benajah Mobley, dec'd, with Moses Maning, Adm'r, & Return same to next Court.

Ordered Road leading from William Hollingsworths to the new Bridge on Cypress Creek be discontinued from where the New Road turns off to the County line.

William Southerland, Hugh McCanne & Moses Maning are appoint- ed a Committee to settle the accounts of the Estate of Benton Williford, dec'd, with James Lanier, Adm'r, & Reporte to next Court.

Reporte of Committee appointed to lay off to Elizabeth Rigby the Widow of William Rigby, dec'd, one years Provisions was returned; Court concurred & Ordered recorded.

James Houston, Redick Worley & ["George" marked through]
William Houston appointed Patrollers in Capt. Houstons Co.

Ordered George Williams Negroes Jim & Amos be taken off the
River & ad[d]ed to William Williams Overseer & work under
him.

Ancrum Shaw Everit, an Orphan now 16 years of age, is bound
Apprentice to John Hunter for & during the next four years &
Nine months to learn the Trade of a Sadler & Harness maker &
to give him six months Schooling.

John Hunter & Joseph Gillespie are appointed Patrollers for
the up[p]er end of Capt. Midletons Co. & David Maxwell & Levi
Mizell for the lower end of said Co.

Court Adjourned Till Court in Course.

[signed] W. Southerland, Edw'd Pearsall, H. McCanne, Jacob
Williams.

<u>15 October, 1804</u> County Court begun & held for County of Duplin
at the Court House, the 3rd Monday.

Present: Worshipfull Edward Pearsall, Esq. who adjourned
Court.

<u>Tuesday Morning [16 Oct 1804]</u> Court met at ten o'clock accord-
ing to adjournment.

Present: Worshipfull James Kenan, James Outlaw, James Pearsall, James Maxwell, Rob't Southerland, Joseph Whitfield,
Esqu'rs.

Samuel Dunn, Andrew Hurst & Elias Faison are appointed a Com-
mittee to settle the accounts of the Estate of George Cooper,
Orphan of George Cooper with James Clark his guardian &
Reporte to Court; Also Ordered that said George Coopers
Receipts shall be good to said James Clark for all such sums
as he will settle for & pay him.

Edward Pearsall, Esq., Jehu Wilkinson, & Andrew McIntire are
appointed a Committee to divide the Estate of William McGowen
& George McGowen, dec'd, so as to ascertain the share of said
Estates coming to Joseph McGowen one of Claimants & Reporte
to next Court.

John Rector, Esq. produced a Licence under hands & Seals of
Spruce Mackay & John L. Taylor, Esq'rs, two of the judges of
the Superior Courts of Law for this State Authorising him the
said John Rector to Practise as an Attorney at Law in the
several County Courts in this State, Whereupon the said John
Rector took Oath for Qualification of Officers & of an
Attorney & took his Seat upon the Bench.

John Hatch Hill is appointed Guardian to Herald Blackmore,
Minor Orphan, he gave Bond of £10,000; Ordered he take his
Estate into his possession.

William Hill is appointed Guardian to Nancy Blackmore, Minor
Orphan, he gave Bond of £10,000; Ordered he take her Estate
into his possession.

Dawson Turner is appointed Overseer of the Road in room of
John Thigpen & to have same District & hands.

Adm'n of Estate of Robert Twilly, dec'd, Granted to Maurice
Moore & Jacob Smith who gave Bond of £1,000 & took Oath of
Adm'rs.

As Charles Hooks, Esq. obtained an Order to remove the Road
between his House & David Hooks, a Jury has been Convened &
now Report that the same is laid off agreeable to Order &
said Road is in sufficient Repair to be Received by the
Overseer.

Read Petition of Sundry Inhabitants praying a Road to be laid
off & opened from the Main Road at the Indian Grave on the
South side of the Grove near John Hunters to run from said
Indian Grave to Isaac Midletons Mill & from thence to the
Main Road at or near John Grimes at or near Stewarts Creek;
Granted.

Ordered James Midleton, Sr., John Best, William Boyet, Sr.,
Jonathan Thomas, Arthur Boyet, John Boyet, George Gibbons,
Thomas Phillips, John Phillips, David Sloan, Joseph Gilles-
pie, David Clark, David Midleton, Edward Armstrong & Richard
Norment, or any 12, be a Jury to view & lay off said Road;
that Peleg Rogers, Constable, summon & convene & Edward
Pearsall, Esq. Qualifie said Jury.

An Instrument in writing signed by William McClure was handed
into Court & proved by David McClure & requested to be Recorded in the words following:

Know all men by these Presents that I do hereby certifie that
the little Sorrel Mare known by the Name of flie was given to
my son John McClure soon after she was foaled & has ever
since been his property, so that I have neither Claim, Right,
nor Title in the same, as Witness my hand this 14th day of
June 1803. William McClure; Test. David McClure.

Thomas Wells is appointed Overseer of the Road in room of
William Brown in the District of Road from John Williams up
to Stewarts Creek & have same hands that William Brown had.

Jacob Monk, Hardy Carleton, William Brown & John Stallings
are appointed Patrollers in District of Capt. Thomas Wells
Co.

Matthew Ward, one of Ex'rs of last Will & Testament of Jesse
Ellison dec'd, (Recorded last Term), Qualified as Ex'r.

Ordered Ex'r of Jesse Ellison, dec'd, sell so much of said
Estate as will pay Debts agreeable to Will & make Return to
next Court.

Grand Jury sworn: William McGee, foreman, Stephen Jones,
John Watkins, Thomas Cole, John Cooper, Benjamin Best, Daniel
Kenan, Jesse Swinson, William McGowen, William Kornegay,

Thomas Sheppard, Thomas Heath, Henry Newkirk, Benjamin
Dulany, Elias Faison.

Ordered Thomas Evens, Constable attend Grand Jury.

Burwell Branch is appointed Overseer of the Road in room of
Solomon Jones & to have same District & hands.

Jeremiah Bennet is appointed a Constable in room of Timothy
Spence resigned, he gave Bond.

Daniel Glisson, George Duncan & Bazil Kornegay are appointed
a Committee to settle Estate of Jacob Kornegay, dec'd with
William Duncan & John Kornegay, Adm'rs & Reporte to next
Court.

James Wright, William Beck, Jr. & ["William" marked out]
Jesse Gully are appointed a Committee to settle the accounts
of Estate of Robert Byrd, dec'd, with Thomas Wright & Robert
Byrd, Ex'rs & Reporte to Court.

Bazil Kornegay, Jacob Kornegay & John Kornegay are appointed
a Committee to settle accounts of Estate of David Peale,
dec'd, with Bryan Minshew, Adm'r, & Reporte to next Court.

Last Will & Testament of William Benett dec'd was Exhibited &
proved by Owen Connerly, one of subscribing witnesses & at
same time David Wright, one of Ex'rs named in said Will,
Qualified.

Deed: John Kingsburry to Simon Totvine[?] dated 22 Feb. 1787
for 4800 acres in the State of Tennessee, formerly or now in
the County of Davidson, proved by James Daniel, one of the
subscribing witnesses.

Sale of Estate of Abigal Parker, dec'd, Exhibited by William
McCanne amounting to £10-14-4; Ordered recorded.

Bryan Bowden, David Wright & Joseph Dickson are appointed a
Committee to settle accounts of Estate of William Gully, Jr.,
dec'd, with Executors & Reporte to next Court.

Luke Kornegay is appointed Guardian to Henry Kornegay, Minor
Orphan, he gave Bond of £2000; Ordered he take his Estate
into his possession, etc.

Bryan Kornegay is appointed Guardian to Penelope Kornegay,
Minor Orphan, he gave Bond of £2000; Ordered he take her
Estate into his possession, etc.

A Jury having been appointed to lay off a New Road from the Old Road at Laniers path below his Mill Swamp to the Lake fourd of Cypress Creek & from thence into the old Wilmington Road at or near the three mile Meadow, have laid off said Road agreeable to said Order.

James Lanier, Sr. is appointed Overseer of said new Road & the following hands work under him: Benjamin Lanier, Dawson Pickett, Nath'l Scarborough, Benjamin Scarborough, Isom Lanier, Jesse Lanier, Stephen Lanier, Jacob Johnston, Charles Pearse, Francis Pickett, John Dale, Isaac Dale, Lewis Dale & Adam Dale.

Luke Kornegay is appointed Overseer of the Road in room of Martin Kornegay & have same District & hands.

Ordered Adm'rs of Robert Twilly dec'd sell Estate of said dec'd & return to next Court.

James Gufford is appointed Overseer of the Road in room of William Kornegay, Jr. & have same District & hands & that Lewis Glisson & David Carter be taken off the River & work under said James Gufford.

Ordered Daniel Glissons hands work on the River under Isaac Kornegay.

Account of Sale of Estate of Jacob Mainor, dec'd, Exhibited by Charity Mainor, Adm'x; Ordered recorded.

Wednesday Morning [17 Oct 1804] Court met at ten o'clock according to adjournment.

Present: Worshipfull James Kenan, Joseph T. Rhodes, James Wright, Daniel Glisson, William Duncan, James Maxwell, Shadrack Stallings, Esquires.

James Dickson, Esq., Benjamin Lanier, Esq., Hugh McCanne, Esq., William Duncan, Esq., Jacob Williams, Esq., Sampson Grimes, Esq., David Williams, Esq., Daniel Glisson, Esq. Returned lists of Taxable for this year 1804.

A Jury having been convened to lay off to [blank] the Widow of John Woodward, dec'd, the Dower of her dec'd husbands lands, have proceeded & Reporte as follows: Beginning at a pine the old corner running thence with the old line S 73 E 68 pole to a pine on the old line, thence N 11 E the new dividing line 114 pole to a Scrub Oak, thence S 83 W 53 pole to

a lightwood Stump & Stake, at or near the last corner of the
50 acre survey, thence with the given line of the said 50
acres survey to a pine the beginning corner of said Survey,
thence S 15 E 170 pole to a pine, Twilleys Corner, thence S 4
W 40 pole to a pine, John Southerlands Corner, thence with
his line E to the beginning, Containing by Estimation 80
acres;   Court concurred & Ordered Recorded.

Read Petition of Sundry Persons praying to have a New Road
laid off to lead from the old Wilmington Road below Island
Creek to the NorthEast River at Cooks old landing (now commonly called Murrays landing), a distance of about three
miles;   Granted.

Ordered the Road leading from William Hollingsworths to the
up[p]er Bridge on Cypress Creek be Revived & that John Halso
be Overseer as formerly & that the following work under him:
Hosea Lanier, John Lanier, James Lanier, Jr., Alexander Mere-
dith, Enoch Parker, John Ranier, Jacob Lanier, Benjamin Padget & Enoch Simpson.

Thomas Evens is appointed a Constable & has given Bond.

Samuel Davis has leave to turn the Road that leads from
Burncoat to Whitfields ferry, leaving the old Road at said
Davis's & to join it again at the end of James Matthews
laine, the said Road being ready Cut open & revived by the
Overseer.

Ordered Thomas Cole, Overseer of the Road leading from Staffords Swamp to Picketts landing do take into his Care & work
the New Road with the same hands from Muddy Creek bridge into
the aforesaid Road lately laid off by a Jury appointed for
that purpose.

As the Court has Granted a New Road laid off from Wilmington
Road near Island Creek to lead to Cooks old landing, Ordered
following be a Jury to view & lay off said new Road & return
a Plan thereof to next Court: James Murray, Asa Murray,
Isaac James, Kainor James, George Powell, Thomas Evens,
Daniel Teachey, John Sloan, Joseph Hodgeson, John Whitman,
Jr., John Mallard, Jr., Henry Hulet, Andrew Thally, John
Carr, William Carr & Jesse Norris or any twelve & that Thomas
Evens, Constable, summon & convene & Timothy Teachy, Esq.
Qualifie said Jury.

Thomas McGee, ["Hugh Maxwell & James Frederick" marked out],
having been appointed & served as Patroller in this Co. for
1802, now allowed 40/ for said service.

As several Judgements have been obtained against Southy Raphel & Executions issued thereon were levied on land & the Sale thereof forbid by Andrew Gufford; Ordered that the Sheriff convene a Jury upon premises to try the property of said disputed land & that he act therein as Law directs.

Ordered Elijah Smith shall work on the Newbern Road under James Williams, Overseer.

Ordered Burrel Williams work on the Soracta Road under Bently Weston, Overseer.

Read Petition of sundry Persons respecting a Road laid off from the New Meeting house on Staffords Swamp to the Newbern Road in Jones Co. at or near Stills Shop etc., praying an alteration in the said Road as follows, to continue the same Road from its beginning as it is now Cut open to the North Prong of Muddy Creek then a direct Course to John Wallers Mill on Limestone Creek & from thence into the Newbern Road at or near the Foard of Thigpens Swamp; Granted.

Nathan Waller is appointed Overseer of said New Road & is to have same hands as were appointed to open & work on said New Road.

Thursday Morning [18 Oct 1804] Court met at ten o'clock according to adjournment.

Present: Worshipfull James Kenan, James Outlaw, Hugh McCanne, Edward Pearsall, Esquires.

Read Petition of sundry Persons praying a New Road to be laid off from Prospect Meeting House in this Co. to Lenoir Co. line near Job Larreys; Granted.

Ordered following be a Jury to view & lay off said new Road & Reporte a Plan thereof to next Court: Alexander Graddy, Fred'k Graddy, Henry Graddy, Thomas Graddy, Sam'l Davis, James Matthews, Edward Alberson, David Alberson, Alex'r Outlaw, Edward Outlaw, John Outlaw, Jonathan Keithly, Alexander Keaton, Jacob Meeks or any twelve; Edward Outlaw, Constable, to summon & convene & James Outlaw, Esq., to Qualifie said Jury.

John Hunter is appointed Standard Keeper of Weights & Measures in this County & is to give Bond & Qualifie.

Reporte of a Settlement of the Estate of James Chambers,
dec'd, with Jeremiah Pearsall, Adm'r, was rendered; Court
concurred & Ordered Recorded.

James Hall, Esq. Sheriff rendered his list of Insolvents for
1803 which were as follows: [all were allowed one Poll]
Holden McGee, Philip Coley, William Murphy, William Goff,
Thomas Jinkins, Charles Williamson, Daniel Holland, William
Folson, Jordan Pennington, Noel Pennington, Adam Greenfield,
Jesse Butler, Thomas Ritter, Thomas Brady, Turner Forte,
Bezant Brock, Isaiah Rogers, Ralph Jernigan, Arkis Ellison,
Hezekiah Blizzard, Elijah Bowen, John Grimes, Jonathan
Nickins, William Street, William Rogers, John Holden, Jacob
Allen, Nathan Rouse, Vincent Carter, Elijah Tucker, Elisha
Carrol, Felix Merrit; Ordered said list recorded & filed in
the Clerks Office.

Gibson Sloan & Robert Southerland, Esquires Returned their
lists of Taxables for this year.

Robert Sloan is appointed Overseer of the Road from Thomas
Heaths to Island Creek Meeting House in room of Amos
Shuffield.

Ordered John Bryan & Son & John Thally be ad[d]ed to John
Sloan Overseer from Maxwell to Island Creek, also William
Rouse is to be taken from John Gilmans Co & ad[d]ed to John
Sloan, Overseer & work under him.

Ordered John Maxwell & Jacob Wells, Jr. on Island Creek are
ad[d]ed to the New Road and work under Robert Sloan, Overseer.

Ordered Sheriff convene a Jury to lay off the Dower of the
lands of William Rigby, dec'd to Elizabeth Rigby, Widow of
said dec'd & make return to next Court.

William Hill & John Cooper, Jr. are appointed Patrols for
up[p]er part of Capt. Pearsalls Co.

Deed: John Dickson to James Harrell for 450 acres, proved by
Edward Armstrong; Ordered registered.

Deed: Jesse Reeves to George Kornegay for 466 acres, proved
by Bazill Kornegay; Ordered registered.

Deed: Hugh McCanne, late Sheriff, to Jehu Wilkinson for 99
acres, Acknowledged; Ordered registered.

Deed: Hugh McCanne, late Sheriff, to William Frederick for
75 acres, Acknowledged; Ordered registered.

Deed: James Willson to Joseph Brooks for 110 acres in two
pieces, proved by Levi Mizell; Ordered registered.

Deed: Thomas Lanier to Isaac Hall for 100 acres, Acknowledged; Ordered registered.

Deed: Jesse Pipkin to Archelaus Pipkin for 185 acres in two
pieces, proved by Alex'r Keaton; Ordered registered.

Deed: John Cooper, Jr. to David Midleton for 130 acres in
two pieces, Acknowledged; Ordered registered.

Deed: Jacob Boney to Jacob Wells for 237 acres, proved by
William Boney; Ordered registered.

Deed: Thomas Prowse to William Underhill for 100 acres,
proved by Jesse Swinson; Ordered registered.

Bill of Sale: Benjamin Ellis to Frederick Smith for a Negro
Peter, proved by Jacob Williams; Ordered registered.

Bill of Sale: Lewis Hicks to Jacob Williams for two Negro
Slaves & Wench named Violet & a Child named Toni, Acknowledged; Ordered registered.

Bill of Sale: William Kornegay to Frederick Smith for a
Negro girl Annia, proved by Loftis Worley; Ordered registered.

Bill of Sale: Hugh McCanne, Sheriff to William Higgins for a
Negro Woman Esther, Acknowledged; Ordered registered.

Bill of Sale: James Price to Andrew Thally for a Negro woman
Flora, proved by Thomas Cumings; Ordered registered.

Following are appointed Jurymen to next Court: John Huffham,
William Stoakes, Thomas Wells, Joseph Brice, Jacob Boney,
John Thally, John Gilman, Moses Maning, Nathan Fountain,
James Newton, Peter Frederick, Benj'n Hodges, Thomas Wright,
Tobias Southerland, John Thigpen, James Pickett, Andrew
McIntire, Jehu Wilkinson, James McGowen, James Midleton,
William Hall, Jr., Hogan Hunter, William Bush, John Cooper,
Jr., Jeremiah Pearsall, Howell Best, Caleb Quinn, Christopher
Lawson, Edward Alberson, Fred'k Graddy, Jr., Stephen Gufford,
Hezekiah Millard, John Kornegay, James Grimes, Edward Winders
& John Beck.

Merrit Manning is allowed 16/ for attending Court as Constable two days this Term.

Thomas Evens is allowed 16/ for attending Court as Constable
two days this Term.

Ordered Grand Jury have Tickets for two days each this Term.

Ordered Petit Jury that served this Term have Tickets for two days each: Robert Bishop, Daniel Murphy, Stephen Williams, William Johnston, Isaac Midleton, David Midleton, John Carr, John Stallings, & Stephen Herring.

James Kenan, James Wright, & James Pearsall are appointed a Committee to view & Inspect the Jail of this Co. & Contract with workmen at their Discretion to make the Necessary Repairs as they may think proper & Render their account for said work to next Court.

Following are appointed Inspecters of the Poll in the ensuing Election for an Elector to vote for President & Vice President of the United States:
The Election to be held at Stanleys - Bazil Kornegay & John Watkins
The Election to be held at Bryans - John Hall & David Boney
The Election to be held at D. Williams - John Stallings & John Hufham
The Election to be held at the Court House - John Hunter & William Dickson, Jr.

Following are appointed Jurymen To Wilmington Superior Court the 13th Nov. next: Bryan Farrior, Joseph Williams (R.F.), Samuel Houston, David Hooks, William Beck, Jr., Gibson Sloan & William Higgins.

James Hall, Esq. produced a Certificate of his being appointed by the last County Court, Sheriff of this County for ensuing year, which Certificate is attested by James Kenan, Esq., Chairman of this Court & the said James Hall has taken Oath of Sheriff & is to give Bond.

Court Adjourned Till Court in Course.

[signed] J. Pearsall, Edw'd Pearsall, H. McCanne

21 January 1805 County Court begun & held for County of Duplin at the Court House, the 3rd Monday.

Present: Worshipful Edward Pearsall, Esq. who adjourned Court.

<u>Tuesday Morning [22 Jan 1805]</u> Court met at 9 o'clock according
to adjournment.

Present: Worshipful James Kenan, James Pearsall, James
Wright, Daniel Glisson, James Maxwell, Sampson Grimes, Hugh
McCanne, Esquires.

Samuel Dunn, James Clark, Isom Faison, Felix K. Hill &
Charles Hooks are appointed a Committee to divide the Real
Estate of Hillary Hooks, dec'd, between the two Claimants
David Hooks & James Hooks, sons of said dec'd.

Aaron Hodgeson, appointed, Qualified & served as a Patroller
for 1799 is now allowed 40/ for said services.

Grand Jury sworn: Thomas Wright, foreman, John Beck, Jehu
Wilkinson, James Grimes, Frederick Graddy, John Thigpen,
Hogan Hunter, James Pickett, John Kornegay, Jeremiah Pear-
sall, William Stoakes, Thomas Wells, James Newton.

Ordered Samuel Herring, Constable, attend Grand Jury.

Merrit Manning is appointed a Constable for ensuing year;
Ordered Clerk take his Bond.

Thomas Kenan, James Wright & Benjamin Johnston are appointed
a Committee to divide lands of John Torrans, dec'd, between
the legal Claimants & return same to next Court.

Ordered Enoch Simpson be cleared from working on Public roads
and mustering in future.

Michael Boney is appointed Overseer of the Road in room of
Elisha Williford & have same District & hands.

State of North Carolina, Duplin County - This day Personally
appeared before me Maurice Fennel & being duly sworn on the
Holy Evangelist of Almighty God deposith & sayeth that he,
said Fennell, drew a Bill of Sale from John Bell to Edward
Rollins for a certain Negro by the name of Bristo and wit-
nessed the same as a Warantee Bill of Sale on the second day
of the Present Month - 22d January 1805. Signed Maurice
Fennel. Sworn before Cha. Hooks, J.P.

John Miller is appointed Guardian to the Orphan Children of
Robert Miller, dec'd, towit, Betsey, Mary, Kitty, Jenney &
Dolly Miller & hath given Bond of £500.

James Bowden is appointed Overseer of the Road in room of
Lewis Jones & to have same District & hands.

Bryan Farrior is appointed Overseer of the Road in room of
Jacob Brown, Jr. & to have same District & hands.

James Kenan, Charles Hooks & Jehu Wilkinson are appointed a
Committee to divide the Estate of John Molten, dec'd, between
the Heirs, towit, William Peacock who claims in right of his
wife & Thomas Molten & to make return to next Court.

Nathan Womble is appointed Guardian to the Orphan Children of
Michael Lobar, dec'd, towit, Mary Lobar, Sarah Lobar & Lewis
Lobar, he gave Bond of £800 for each etc.   pd 18/.

David Alberson is appointed a Constable, he gave Bond.

William Beck, County Surveyor, Resigned said appointment;
Acccepted.

Edward Pearsall, Charles Hooks & William Beck are appointed a
Committee to settle Accounts of Estate of Thomas Norment,
dec'd, with Ex'rs & return to this Court.

David Sloan, charged with begeting a Bastard Child of Char-
lotte Brinson, gave Bond required by law.

Bazill Kornegay is appointed Surveyor for this County & is
Qualified as such in Court; Ordered Clerk take his Bond.

Upon Petition of Susannah Carter for an allowance for maintenance of her Child Bently Stewart. Court allowed her £23;
Ordered Notice issue to Bently Weston to appear at next Court
to show Cause if any why Execution should not issue against
him for same, he being bound for said Childs maintenance,
etc.

Andrew McIntire, John Wilkinson & William McGee are appointed
a Committee to divide the Estate of James James, dec'd, so as
to ascertain the share thereof coming to Gabriel James, one
of the Heirs & Claimants, agreeable to Will of said dec'd &
Reporte to Court.

Bazill Kornegay tenders for his Securities as Surveyor,
Daniel Glisson, William Duncan, David Kornegay & Jonathan
Thomas who are approved.

As a Tax of three pence has been laid for Building a bridge
over Rockfish Creek & is not yet collected & is found to be
inadequate for said purpose, Ordered Clerk certifie to
Sheriff that he is hereby Ordered & directed to collect for
that purpose a four penney Tax instead of a three penny Tax.

John Matthis & John Shuffield for Reasons rendered to Court
are Exempted from bearing Arms at Musters & from working on
Public Roads in the future.

Ordered Sitation issued to Thomas Findley, Guardian to
Orphans of Charles Brown, dec'd, to appear before the next
Court prepared to settle his Accounts of said Guardianship,
etc.

Adm'n of Estate of Nancy Houston, dec'd, granted Frederick
Sowell who Qualified & offers as Securities Samuel Sowell &
Phill Southerland, Jr. who are approved; Ordered Clerk take
his Bond in sum of £500.

Jesse Gully is appointed Guardian to James Gully & Henry
Gully, Orphans of William Gully, dec'd & hath given Bond of
£500 for both; Ordered he take their Estates into Possession. pd 6/.

James Dickson, Sr., Edward Pearsall, Esquires, Benjamin Best,
George Gibbons & John Cooper, Jr. are appointed a Committee
to divide the lands of William Rigby, dec'd, amongst the
several Heirs Claiming same, and that Amos Johnston be
appointed Surveyor to said Committee; Also said Committee,
or any three, be appointed to divide the Personal Estate of
said William Rigby to the said Heirs & Reports to next Court.

William Chasten is appointed a Constable for ensuing year &
has Qualified; Ordered Clerk take his Bond.

Joseph Whitfield, Stephen Jones & Willis Hines with County
Surveyor are appointed a Committee to run & ascertain the
lines of 290 acres of Estate of Jacob Kornegay, dec'd, lying
on the No. side of the NorthEast & to ascertain whether the
said land holds out the full Compliment & to divide said land
equally between Henry Kornegay, Penney Kornegay & Mary
Kornegay agreeable to a former Reporte & Return same to
Court.

Elizabeth Rigby is appointed Guardian to her five Children,
Orphans of William Rigby, dec'd, towit, Bryant, Russell,
Kitty, Beckey & Fanny Rigby & hath given Bond in £2000;
Ordered she take their Estates into her possession.

["Peter Carleton & John Maxwell appointed" marked through.]

Bryan Kornegay is appointed Guardian to Mary Kornegay, a
Minor & hath given Bond of £1000; Ordered he take her Estate
into his possession.

William Matthis is appointed a Constable for ensuing year;
Ordered he give Bond.

Joseph Whitfield, Stephen Jones & Willis Hines appointed a
Committee to settle accounts of Estate of Jacob Kornegay,
dec'd, with Guardian of Henry, Penny & Mary Kornegay &
Reporte to next Court.

Wednesday Morning [23 Jan 1805] Court met at 9 o'clock
according to adjournment.

Present: Worshipfull James Kenan, James Outlaw, James
Wright, James Maxwell, James Dickson, Robert Southerland,
Cha. Hooks, Shad'k Stallings, Jacob Williams, Hugh McCanne,
William Duncan, William Beck, Sampson Grimes & William
Southerland, Esquires.

Daniel Kenedy is appointed Overseer of the Road from Benjamin
Rhodes to Soracta in room of James Williams & have same
District & hands.

Ordered Tax of 1/ & 6 pence on each & every Poll Taxable & on
each & every 300 acres in this County be levied & Collected
for 1804 for County Contingencies, etc.

William Dickson, Clerk of this Court, is allowed £20 as usual
for Extra Services for 1804.

James Hall, Esq. Sheriff of this County, is allowed £35 for
his services as Sheriff for last year, 1804.

James Wright, Samuel Dunn & Charles Hooks are appointed a
Committee to examine & settle accounts of Thomas Kenan,
Guardian to Orphans of Thomas James, & Reporte to next Court.

Darling Daffin is appointed Overseer of the old Cypress Creek
Road from Wm Hollingsworths to New Hanover County line & have
same hands that formerly worked under Wm Johnston & that
William Picketts Sam be ad[d]ed to his District.

Charles Hooks, James Wright & James Midleton, Sr. are ap-
pointed a Committee to settle the accounts of the Estate of
William Rigby, dec'd, between the Widow & the Orphans &
Reporte to next Court.

Ordered John Maxwell & his hands be taken off the New Road &
that they work on the old Road under David Quinn, Overseer.

Ordered Joseph Thomas Rhodes hands work on the Road where
Nathan Waller is Overseer.

Ordered Archibald Thomas & Samuel Whaley work on Road where Matthew Sumner is Overseer.

Ordered William Whaley, Sr., William Whaley, Jr. & William Baisden & their hands work on the Road from New River to Jones Co. line.

As a Road has been laid off from the old Wilmington Road below Island Creek to Asa Murrays landing on the NorthEast, Ordered George Powell be Overseer of said New Road & that Walter Bryan, Frederick Bowen, Nicanor Murray, John Whitman, Reuben Norris, Isom Norris, David Whitman, Benjamin Bratcher, Jehu Cook & Edward Street work under him on said Road.

Ordered that the Road that was Ordered at last July Term to lead from Laniers Swamp crossing Cypress Creek & into the Wilmington Road at or near the Three Mile Meadow, be turned off from that direction & to go the way that is already laid off & opened by consent of the hands that is to work thereon - to lead near to Snowden Pearses Plantation and into the Wilmington Road at or near the branch called Cooks Well.

Ordered Ex'rs of Thomas Normant, dec'd, sell a further part of Perishable Estate sufficient to meet Demands which now to their knowledge is likely to come against said Estate & Return same to next Court.

Ordered Frederick Sowell, Adm'r of Nancy Houston, dec'd, sell Estate of said Dec'd & make return to next Court.

Ordered a New Road be laid off from the North Prong of Muddy Creek to the Newbern Road at or near the foard of Thigpens Swamp & that Jesse Brown, John Waller, Charles Bostick, Joseph T. Rhodes, William Hunter, Edward Hunter, Job Padget, John Thigpen, Thomas Kenedy, Robert Bishop, Sr., Robert Harris, Arch'd Thomas, Reuben Nethercut & Laban Williams, or any twelve, be a Jury to view & lay off said Road & Return a Plan to next Court.

And that Phill Southerland, Constable, summon & convene & that Robert Southerland, Esq. Qualifie said Jury.

Ann Dickson is appointed Guardian to her Children, Minors & Orphans of Edward Dickson, dec'd, towit, Jones, Hannah, Sarah & Robinson Dickson, she gave Bond of £5,000 for the whole of them; Ordered she take their Estates into possession.

Ordered Ann Dickson, Widow of Edward Dickson, dec'd, & Guardian of the four minor Orphans of said dec'd, shall keep as she has done since her Husbands death, all the Negroes

belonging to the Estate of said Edward Dickson, dec'd, in
her possession & have the labour of said Negroes as a full
compensation for the maintenance & Schooling of the four
Minor Orphans of said dec'd, towit, Jones, Hannah, Sarah &
Robinson Dickson until Court shall otherwise direct.

Edward Pearsall, James Hall & Andrew McIntire are appointed a
Committee to settle the accounts of the Estate of Edward
Dickson, dec'd between Jehu Wilkinson, the Adm'r, & Ann Dick-
son, the Guardian of the Children & Reporte to next Court.

David Carleton, Gibson Sloan & Obadiah Wade with the County
Surveyor be a Committee to divide the lands of James Huggins,
dec'd, between the Several Heirs who Claim their distributive
share, towit, Sarah Stricklin, Elinor Hines, Elizabeth Huggins & Solomon Huggins & Reporte a plan to next Court & that
Peleg Rogers, Constable, convene said Committee & County
Surveyor upon the Premises.

The Stray Master made a return of following Strays:
Jacob Brown, Jr. a Heifer valued to $3, Entered the 1st
January, 1804; David Wright, a small Stear valued to $5,
Entered the 1st Jan., 1804
Signed, Robert Southerland, Ranger;
Ordered Clerk Reporte same according to law.

Account of amount of Negro hire of the Heirs of Edward Blackmore, dec'd, amounting to £269-7-6 Exhibited by William Hill,
Adm'r; Ordered recorded.

Reporte of Committee on settlement of Estate of David Peale,
dec'd, Rendered; Court concurred & Ordered recorded.

Reporte of Committee on division of Estate of John Molten,
dec'd, between William Peacock & Thomas Molten Exhibited;
Court concurred & Ordered recorded.

James Dickson, Jr. Petitioned to build a Public Grist Mill on
the Run of Grove Swamp where he is Owner of land on one side
& the Heirs of William Rigby, dec'd, on the other; Granted.

Account of the Sales of the Estate of Robert Twilley, dec'd,
amounting to $1,140.04 was Exhibited by Maurice Moore & Jacob
Smith, Adm'rs; Ordered recorded.

John Burnham is exempted in future from payment of a Poll Tax
for self.

Inventory of Estate of William Bennit, dec'd, Exhibited by
David Wright, Ex'r; Ordered recorded.

Ordered Hugh McCanne, late Sheriff of Duplin Co., be allowed
in his settlement with County Trustee for 1802 the sum of
£13-5-8 for amount of sundry mistakes & overcharged in list
of Taxables during the Term of his being Sheriff.

Inventory of Estate of Nancy Houston, dec'd, Exhibited by
Frederick Sowell, Adm'r; Ordered filed & recorded.

Reporte of Committee on settlement of Estate of Thomas
Norment, dec'd, Exhibited; Ordered recorded.

Reporte of Committee on settlement of Estate of William
Gully, dec'd, Exhibited; Court concurred & Ordered recorded.

Account of Sale of Estate of William Bennit, dec'd, amounting
to £352-2-2 Exhibited by David Wright, Ex'r; Ordered
recorded.

Post Inventory of Estate of William Rigby, dec'd, Exhibited;
Ordered recorded.

Account of Sale of Estate of Robert Miller, dec'd, Exhibited;
Ordered recorded.

Reporte of Committee on settlement of Estate of Robert Byrd,
dec'd, with the Ex'r Exhibited; Ordered recorded.

Frederick Graddy of Lenoir County is appointed Overseer of
the Road in room of Henry Graddy & to have same District &
hands & that William Graddy, Fred'k Graddy, Sr., Allen
Graddy, Sr., Henry Graddy & Theophilus Williams work under
him.

Ordered following: John Hunter, James Frederick, Hugh
Maxwell, Robert Sloan, Thomas McGee, William Hall, William
Johnston, Howell Best, Stephen Brown, James Winders, James
Ward, David Wright, Daniel Kenan, Mark Rogers, John Watkins,
Lewis Jones, George J. Hodom, Edward Winders, James Grimes,
William Kornegay, Jr., Alex'r O'Daniel, Jonathan Keithly,
Sam'l Houston, George Houston, Richard Swinson, Rob't Bishop,
Sr., Tobias Southerland, Lewis Davis, Moses Maning, Nathan
Fountain, Jacob Lanier, John Gilman, Daniel Murphy, Isom
Norris, Stephen Williams, Samuel Davis, Abraham Newton,
William Swetman, Henry Porter & Hardy Carleton be Jurymen
next Court.

Ordered Grand Jury have Tickets for one day each this Term.

Sam'l Herring is allowed 8/ for attending Court as Constable
one day this Term.

Merrit Maning is allowed 16/ for attending Court two days
this Term.

Ordered Clerk to record all Deeds & Bills of Sale etc. which
have been Acknowledged & proved in Court this Term after the
Adjournment of the Court, also all Orders concerning Roads,
etc.

Court Adjourned till Court in Course.

[signed]   J. Pearsall, James Dickson, Hugh McCanne.

Minutes of January Term, 1805 continued.   [Day & date not
given.]

As an Order of last October Term a New Road was Ordered to
be laid off from Prospect Meeting House in this County to
Lenoir County near Job Learys, a Jury has been convened &
Reporte that they have proceeded & have laid out the said New
Road agreeable to said Order.

Ordered Alexander Carter be Overseer of said New Road & that
Edward Carter, Manuel Carter, Laurence Thomson, James Stewart, Daniel Stewart, Joshua Stewart, Benjamin Deaver, Alexander Deaver, John Ward, John Quinney, Isaac Dawson, Jr.,
Joseph Dawson & Daniel Boyet work under him.

Ordered Road where Benjamin Hodges is Overseer be divided
into two separate Districts. That one District shall be from
the Edge of Goshen Swamp through Mrs. Herrings laine & to
Middle of Run of Bear Swamp; & that Alexander Herring be
Overseer & that his own hands, Widow Herrings, Stephen
Herrings, Benj'n Hodges, James Rhodes & Auston Morris hands
work under him.

Ordered the other District of said Road shall be from the Run
of Reedy branch to the Arm Post in Widow Herrings laine &
from thence to the Run of Horsepen branch at Maurice Moores &
that David Wright be Overseer of said District & that his own
hands & Widow Wrights, Elisha Herrings, Maurice Moores & the
hands on Lewis Dicksons Plantation work under him.

Bill of Sale: Owen Kenan to Isaac Wright for a Negro man
Jim, proved by Andrew McIntire; Ordered registered.

Bill of Sale: Hillary Whitehurst to Benjamin Beat for a
Negro boy Gabe, proved by Owen Rigby; Ordered registered.

Bill of Sale: Mills Godwin to Jeremiah Pearsall for a Negro woman Trease, proved by Shadrack Stallings; Ordered registered.

Bill of Sale: John James, Edward Dickson, Thomas James & Edward Pearsall to Hannah Johnston for a Negro girl Hannah, Acknowledged by Edward Pearsall; Ordered registered.

Bill of Sale: John Bell to Thomas Bell for a Negro Brister, Acknowledged; Ordered registered.

Bill of Sale: Jehu Wilkinson to John Thally for a Negro woman Silvia, Acknowledged; Ordered registered.

Bill of Sale: James Hall to John Thally for a Negro woman Penny, Acknowledged; Ordered registered.

Plan of Dower of lands of William Rigby, dec'd, laid off for Elizabeth Rigby, the Widow, was returned by Amos Johnston, the Surveyor & signed by the Jury as follows: Beginning at a Sweet Gum at the Run of the Grove Swamp & runs S 5 E 212 pole to a Bay on Horse branch, thence down the Meanders of same as far as will make 92 pole on a straight line, thence N 5 W 55 pole to a stake by the fence in the field, thence S 85 W 13 1/2 pole, thence down the fence Row N 8 E 108 pole to the Run of Grove Swamp & thence up same to beginning, Containing for Dower 123 acres.

Deed: William Dickson to Lewis Dickson for 230 acres, Acknowledged; Ordered registered.

Deed: Parham Puckett to Austin Beesly for 100 acres, proved by Jacob Matthis; Ordered registered.

Deed: William Jones to Henry Cook for 200 acres, proved by Leonard Mills; Ordered registered.

Deed: Robert Greeves to Leven Watkins for 125 acres, proved by John Watkins; Ordered registered.

Deed: Henry Hollingsworth to William Hollingsworth for 267 acres, proved by William Pickett; Ordered registered.

Deed: Jacob Matthis to Auston Beesley for 73 acres, proved by Jacob Mathis; Ordered registered.

Deed: James Wright to Isaac Wright for 550 acres, Acknowledged; Ordered registered.

Deed: Auston Beesley to Parham Puckett for 120 acres, Acknowledged; Ordered registered.

Deed: John Sulliven to Hampton Sulliven for 155 acres,
proved by Henry Graddy; Ordered registered.

Deed: Charles R. Johnston to William Beck for sundry lands,
proved by William Beck, Sr.; Ordered registered.

Deed: Lewis Martin to Willis Hines for 300 acres, proved by
George Thomas; Ordered registered.

Deed: John Fellow to Elijah Powell for 35 acres, proved by
John Matthis; Ordered registered.

Deed: William Jones to Lewis Gardner for 75 acres, proved by
Thomas Butler; Ordered registered.

Deed: William James to William James, Jr. for sundry lands,
proved by Aaron Williams; Ordered registered.

Deed: Ben Dullany, Sr. to Thomas Dullany for 100 acres,
Acknowledged; Ordered registered.

Deed: Lewis Graddy to Timothy Graddy for sundry lands,
proved by Henry Graddy, Ordered registered.

Deed: Timothy Wilson to Daniel Alderman for 108 acres,
proved by David Alderman; Ordered registered.

Deed: Benjamin Fussell to William James for 22 acres, proved
by Aaron Williams; Ordered registered.

Deed: David Alderman to Daniel Alderman, Jr. for 40 acres,
Acknowledged; Ordered registered.

Deed: Joel Rogers to Hezekiah Millard for 150 acres, Proved
by Jesse Turnage; Ordered registered.

Deed: John Sulliven to Hampton Sulliven for 88 acres, proved
by Henry Graddy; Ordered registered.

Deed: William James & John James to Benjamin Fussell for 41
acres, proved by William James; Ordered registered.

Deed: Daniel Alderman to David Alderman for 173 acres, Acknowledged; Ordered registered.

Deed: William James to Benjamin Fussell for 221 acres,
proved by Aaron Williams; Ordered registered.

Deed: Shadrack Mills to John Basden for 100 acres, proved by
Ben. Dullaney; Ordered registered.

Deed: James Mills Mumford to Charles Sowell for 240 acres,
proved by Rob't Southerland; Ordered registered.

Deed: Lewis Martin, Nancy Martin, Jedediah Blanshard, Mary
Blanshard, Stephen Hines & Marrinna [Marianna] Hines to
George Thomas for 200 acres, proved by Needham Whitfield;
Ordered registered.

Deed: William Glisson to Alexander O'Daniel for 2 pieces
land, 72 acres, Acknowledged; Ordered registered.

Deed: Jedediah Blanshard to Nathaniel Price for 2 pieces of
land, 100 acres, Acknowledged; Ordered registered.

Deed: Jacob Glisson to William Glisson for 2 pieces of land,
72 acres, proved by John Outlaw; Ordered registered.

Assignment in writing from Kenan Love to James Wright, Thomas
Wright & David Wright, being an Acquital from payment of a
certain Note given by them to Edward Blackmore for £200,
proved by Daniel Glisson & Jehu Wilkinson; Ordered registered.

The foregoing are Minutes of January Term 1805.
Test Wm Dickson, C.C.

<u>15 April 1805</u>   County Court begun & held for County of Duplin
at the Court House, the 3rd Monday.

Present: Worshipfull James Dickson, Edward Pearsall & James
Maxwell, Esquires, who adjourned Court.

<u>Tuesday Morning [16 Apr 1805]</u>   Court met at 10 o'clock according
to adjournment.

Present: Worshipfull William Beck, Daniel Glisson, James
Maxwell, Esquires.

The Last Will & Testament of James Gillespie was Exhibited &
proved by James Midleton & Robert Midleton, two of subscribing witnesses & at the same time David Gillespie & Joseph
Gillespie, Ex'rs named in said Will, Qualified.

Ordered Rachel Johnston, Minor Orphan about eleven years of
age, Bound Apprentice to Phill Southerland till age 18 to
have one years schooling & learn to Spin, etc.

Grand Jury Qualified: Moses Manning, foreman, William John-
ston, James Grimes, ["James Ward" marked through] excused,
Henry Porter, Lewis Davis, William Swetman, Robert Bishop,
James Frederick, Alexander O'Daniel, Jonathan Keithly, Hugh
Maxwell, Nathan Fountain, Lewis Jones, Thomas McGee.

Ordered Thomas Evens, Constable, attend Grand Jury.

Ordered Davis Woodward, Minor Orphan now about 12 years of
age, Bound Apprentice to James Rhodes to have one years
schooling & to learn trade of a Carriage Wheel maker. pd
14/.

Benjamin Fussell is appointed Overseer of the Road from
Rockfish Bridge leading to John Williams in room of William
Boaney & have same District & hands.

Isaac Spence is appointed Overseer of the Road in room of
George Duncan & have same District & hands.

William Waterman is appointed Guardian to Charity Carter a
Minor Orphan & he gave Bond of £1,000; Ordered he take her
Estate into possession.

Andrew McIntire is appointed Overseer of the Road in room of
James Midleton from the ["12"[?] marked through] mile Post as
formerly down to end of the NorthEast Bridge at limestone &
have same District & hands.

Lewis Herring, Daniel Glisson & Edward Alberson are appointed
Patrollers in Co. of John A. Swinsons Co.; Ordered they
Qualifie.

Samuel Dunn is appointed Guardian to Seney Idolet, a Minor,
he gave Bond £1,000 with approved security; Ordered he take
her Estate into Possession.

Tho. Kenan, Bryan Bowden, David Midleton & Alexander Herring
are appointed a Committee to settle the accounts of the Estate of Jacob Idolet, dec'd, with William Burnham & Reporte
to next Court.

Samuel Herring is appointed a Constable for ensuing year & is
to give Bond.

Thomas Wright is appointed Guardian to Isaac Hunter, a Minor,
he gave Bond £15,000; Ordered he take his Estate into Possession, etc.

John Brice being charged with begeting a Bastard Child of
Abigal Smith, has given Bond required by law.

Ordered Sheriff convene a Jury & lay off to Milley Sulliven,
Widow of Michael Sulliven, dec'd, her Dower of her dec'd
Husbands Estate & Return same to next Court.

James Grimes, Archelaus Branch & Solomon Jones with Bazill
Kornegay, County Surveyor be a Committee to divide the Real
Estate of Michael Sulliven, dec'd, amongst the several Heirs
& make Return to next Court.

Milley Sulliven is appointed Guardian to her Children, towit
to Sally Sulliven, Catharin Sulliven, Betsy Sulliven, William
Sulliven & Samuel Sulliven; Ordered she give Bond of £100
for Each & that Clerk take Bonds, etc.

Ordered Milley Sulliven, Adm'x of Michael Sulliven, dec'd,
shall sell the Whole Personal Estate of said dec'd & Reporte
to next Court.

Adm'n of Estate of Anna Houston Granted Frederick Sowell who
gave Bond of £500 & took Oath of Adm'r.

Adm'n of Estate of William Churchwell, dec'd, Granted Sarah
Churchwell who gave Bond of £500 & took Oath of Adm'x.

William Harris is appointed a Constable, he gave Bond.

Jacob Williams & Isaac Kornegay, Esquires, Alexander Graddy,
Henry Graddy & Chris'r Lawson are appointed a Committee to
lay off one years provisions of Estate of William Churchwell,
decd, to his Widow Sarah Churchwell & return same to next
Court.

Sarah Churchwell, Adm'x of William Churchwell, dec'd,
returned an Inventory of said Estate; Ordered recorded.

Ordered Adm'x of William Churchwell, dec'd, sell Estate of
said dec'd & return same to next Court.

Ordered Bently Weston be exonerated from any further Charges
or expences for maintinance of a Bastard called Bently Stewart, son of Susanna Carter; The Court makes this Order on
the Ground or belief of said Childs being the Son of some
Mullatto which appears from Evidence.

Upon Motion of Mr. Jones it is Ordered that the above Order
be Postponed till next Court for Argument & further Proceedings thereon.

Wednesday Morning [17 Apr 1805] Court met at 9 o'clock
according to adjournment.

Present: Worshipfull William Beck, Charles Hooks, Timothy
Teachy, James Outlaw, Hugh McCanne, Esquires.

Shadrack Stallings, Charles Hooks, Leven Watkins, ["Hugh
McCanne" marked through], Edward Armstrong, Timothy Teachy,
Daniel Kenan & John Hall are appointed Jurymen to Wilmington
Superior Court to be held 13th May next.

Joseph T. Rhodes, William Southerland & Nathan Waller are
appointed a Committee to settle with Robert Southerland,
Guardian to Orphans of Elisha Woodward, dec'd & return to
next Court.

As at last October Term 1804, the Case of Jesse George ag't
John Boney was Referred to James Dickson, James Maxwell, Amos
Johnston, Ephraim Powers & Edward Pearsall who returned their
award to January Term last 1805, in which they assessed Damages to £5-0-0 & Costs, & it is now suggested that the Papers
then laid before said Arbitrators to guide their decision in
said Case, were not Correct, & if so, of course the Award
made thereon may be incorrect also: It is therefore Ordered
that the said Arbitrators may Reconsider the Case & for their
information may Refer to any other Papers or Evidence that
either party may lay before them, & Return their Award to
next Court.

An Account between the Commissioners of limestone Bridge &
Hugh McCanne, late Sheriff & Collecter of said Bridge Tax, by
which it appears said Hugh McCanne has expended for said
Bridge £153-2-9, which leaves a ballance due said McCanne to
be paid him out of the Tax to be collected for said Bridge by
James Hall, Sheriff for 1803, of £5-16-4; Ordered said
account recorded & filed.

Reporte of Committee appointed to divide Estate of James
James, dec'd so as to ascertain the Amount of Share coming to
Gabriel James, have returned their Report in writing; It
appears Gabriel James has received a Negro man at $450, there
is Ballance due Gabriel James of $91.51; Ordered recorded.
pd 4/.

Upon motion in favour of Temperance Williams, Widow of Wright
Williams, Court allowed her £25-13-0, being the amount of
property she bo't at the Sale of her de'd Husbands Estate as
a Compensation for her trouble & Expence in Raising & Maintaining the five Children of her dec'd Husband; Ordered
Clerk certifie same.

James Williams is Exonerated from payment of twofold Tax on
500 acres in Mistake Entered as not given in in 1804.

Jesse George suggested there was an error in a Grant or Patent of 50 acres in Duplin Co Granted him 11 Jul 1783 [no.]
989; Ordered County Surveyor Assertain the Error, if any &
Reporte same to next Court.

Ordered Levi Heath, Alexander Heath & William Heath work on
New Road from Island Creek Meeting House to Wm Heaths at the
old Road at Maxwell Creek under Robert Sloan, Overseer.

Ordered Mary Quinn, Widow of James Quinn, dec'd, be allowed
£20 out of Estate of her dec'd Husband for support of her
five children for 1804.

Ordered Elizabeth Rigby, Widow of William Rigby, dec'd, be
allowed £20 for support of her five children out of Estate of
her dec'd Husband for present year 1805.

Willis Hines is appointed Overseer of the Road in room of
Jonathan Keithly & have same District & hands.

Ordered James Hall, Esq., Sheriff, pay Hugh McCanne, late
Sheriff, £5-16-4 out of Tax laid for 1803 for building a
bridge over the North East River at the mouth of limestone,
it being a ballance overpaid Frederick Sowell by said McCanne
more than his part of the Collection of the Tax for 1802 to
build said Bridge.

The Commissioners for Repairing limestone Bridge towit Robert Southerland, Auston Bryan & Hugh McCanne rendered their account for services for ten days each at 10/ per day, amounting to £15; Court allowed.

Ordered Sheriff pay the above sum of £15 to said Robert Southerland, Auston Bryan & Hugh McCanne out of Tax laid for 1803 for building the bridge over the NorthEast River at Mouth of limestone.

Benjamin Lanier, Esq & William Pickett are appointed a Committee to state & settle accounts of Estate of Benajah Mobley between the Widow & Adm'r & Reporte to next Court.

Joseph T. Rhodes, Hugh McCanne & Nathan Waller are appointed a Committee to state & settle accounts of Estate of Jesse Lanier, dec'd, between the Heirs & the Adm'r & Reporte to next Court.

Peter Carleton was appointed & served as Patroller in 1803 & is allowed 40/.

Reporte of division of Estate of William Rigby, dec'd, rendered by Committee appointed by which it appears that each Childs share of Estate, Real & Personal, amounts to £76-3-11; Court concurred & Ordered recorded.

Platt of division of lands of William Rigby, dec'd, was rendered by Bazill Kornegay, the Surveyor; Ordered filed.

Reporte of division of Estate & settlement of accounts of Estate of Wm. Rigby, dec'd, between the different Claimants & the Adm'rs was returned by the Committee appointed by which it appears that the amount of Personal Estate which have come into hands of Adm'rs is   £517-5-0
Expenditures & Commissions of Adm'rs   88-7-3
Ballance in hands of Adm'rs of   £428-17-9
to be divided amongst different Claimants; Court concurred & Ordered recorded.

Account of Sale of Estate of Nancy Houston, dec'd, rendered by Frederick Sowell, the adm'r, amounting to £151-4-4; Ordered recorded.

Account of Sale of Estate of Jesse Ellison, dec'd, rendered by Matthew Ward, Ex'r, amounting to £70-12-0; Ordered recorded.

Reporte of the Committee of the division of the lands of Hillary Hooks, dec'd, rendered; Court concurred & Ordered recorded.

["Reporte of Committee appointed to divide & assertain the
lines of 200 acres of Estate of Jacob Kornegay, dec'd,
divided amongst three of the Heirs, to wit Pennelope, Henry &
Mary, rendered by Bazill Kornegay, the Surveyor & one of the
said Committee, Court approved & Ordered recorded." marked
through.]   Error, Expunged.

Reporte of settlement with Thomas Kenan, Guardian to the
Orphans of Thomas James, dec'd, rendered by which it appears
there is ballance in hands of said Guardian due the Orphans
£371-14-10;   Court concurred & Ordered recorded.

Reporte of division of Estate of William McGowen, dec'd, for
assertaining the share coming to Joseph McGowen, one of the
Claimants, by which it appears the share is £386-8-0;   Court
concurred & Ordered recorded.

Reporte of Committee appointed to divide the Estate of George
McGowen, dec'd, so as to assertain the share coming to Joseph
McGowen, one of the Claimants, was rendered by which it ap-
pears that the Committee have allotted to him a Negro girl
Hagar at £150 & that there is yet a ballance due him of £43;
Court concurred & Ordered recorded.

Reporte of division of lands of John Torrans, dec'd, was
rendered by Committee appointed by which it appears that
there was found only 210 acres to be divided amongst nine
Claimants which is divided into lotts of 23 acres each;
Court concurred & Ordered recorded.

Article of agreement between William Hall, Sr. & John Hall
concerning Saw Mills, etc. was proved by James Hall;   Ordered
registered.

Bond from William Hall, Sr. to John Hall for performance of
sundry Conditions concerning a Saw Mill, etc. was proved by
James Hall;   Ordered registered.

Grand Jury returned a list of Orphans in this County as
objects worthy of attention of the Court, they being desti-
tute, towit: Enoch Quin, Loftis Quin, John Quin, ["Alexander
Quin" marked through], Ellenor Quin & Henrietta Quin, Orphans
of George Quin, dec'd, all in District of Capt. Houstons Co.

Also five or six Orphan Children of John Brown, dec'd, living
with the Widow of said dec'd in Capt. David Williams Co,
being in distress.

Ordered Sheriff Notice the Mother or such Persons as have the
care of said Orphans to bring them to next Court in Order
they may be provided for.

Last Will & Testament of John Neale, dec'd, Exhibited &
proved by Edward Houston & Andrew McIntire, the subscribing
witnesses & at the same time John Neale, one of the Ex'rs
named in said Will, Qualified.

Thomas Evens allowed 8/ for attending Court as Constable one
day this Term.

Love Savage allowed 8/ for attending Court as Constable one
day this Term.

Pursuant to an Order of this Court of last January Term a
Jury has been convened & laid off a New Road from the North
prong of Muddy Creek into the Newbern Road at or near the
foard of Thigpens Swamp, Beginning at said North Prong then
along a Road newly opened, commonly called Wallers Road,
running through John Wallers Plantation, crossing limestone a
little below Wallers Mill, thence the uppermost Edge of
Rhodes Pocosin nearly a direct Course into the Newbern Road
at the brow of the Hill on the South side of Thigpens Swamp;
Court concurred etc.

Read Petition of Sundry Inhabitants on Waters of Rockfish
Creek praying a Road may be laid off Leading out of Sampson
Road at the lower end of the Bay called Harvills Bay & thence
a direct Course down to Abraham Newkirks at the County line,
there to joine a New Road from Washington;   Granted.

Ordered James Newton, Britton Powell, John Alderman, Daniel
Alderman, Enoch Newton, William Hysmith, William Bland, David
Alderman, Jr., Jesse Lee, Elias Sutton, Isaac Newton, David
Alderman, Sr., be a Jury to view & lay off said new Road &
reporte a Plan to next Court.

Ordered John Matthis, Constable, summon & convene & Shadrack
Stallings, Esq. Qualifie said Jury.

["Read Petition of Sundry Inhabitants of Rockfish praying a
New Road be laid off leading from the Main Road at Harvills
Bay the most direct way into the main Road at John Millers[?]
& that the hands on the West side of Rockfish Creek be
granted to open & Maintain the said Road & that Abraham
Newton be appointed Overseer;   Granted" marked through.]
Expunged by Order of the Court.

Bill of Sale: Henry Cotten to Stephen Miller for four
Negroes, Flora, Zibe, Nancy & Davy, proved by John Houston;
Ordered registered.

Bill of Sale: Henry Walters to Jesse Hardy for a Negro wench
Pat & her child Simon, proved by Joseph Elliott; Ordered
registered.

Bill of Sale: John Gibbs to Thomas Bennett for a Negro boy
Toney, Proved by James Watkins; Ordered registered.

Bill of Sale: Thomas Adams to David Cannon for a Negro boy
Moses & an assignment of said Bill of Sale from said David
Cannon to Lewis Carleton, Acknowledged by said David Cannon;
Ordered registered.

Bill of Sale: Jacob Williams to Samuel Stanford for three
Negroes, Ceaser, Moriah & a Child without any name, Acknowledged; Ordered registered.

Bill of Sale: Jesse Hardy to John Waller for a Negro woman
Pat, proved by Nathan Waller; Ordered registered.

Bill of Sale: Caleb Quin to Nathan Waller for a Negro woman
Rachel, proved by Phill Southerland; Ordered registered.

Bill of Sale: Catharine Love to Ben Cooper for a Negro boy
Jack, proved by Benjamin Best; Ordered registered.

Deed: Alexander Saunders to Henry Newkirk for two pieces
land, proved by Rob't Southerland; Ordered registered.

Deed: David Rogers to David Brock for 100 acres, proved by
Jesse Brock; Ordered registered.

Deed: John Williams to Joseph Williams for five pieces of
land, proved by Aaron Williams; Ordered registered.

Deed: John Hunter to Andrew McIntire for 72 acres, Proved by
Jeremiah Pearsall; Ordered registered.

Deed: William Higgins to Benjamin Best for 48 acres, Acknowledged; Ordered registered.

Deed: Benjamin Best to Etheldred Best for 48 acres, Acknowledged; Ordered registered.

Deed: Jehu Wilkinson to William Boyet for 99 acres, proved
by Thomas Wright; Ordered registered.

Deed: Thomas Shelton to Etheldred Best for 55 acres, proved
by Benjamin Best; Ordered registered.

Deed: John Cooper to Thomas Shelton for 53 acres, proved by
Benjamin Best; Ordered registered.

Deed: James Clark to Samuel Dunn for 828 acres, Acknowledged; Ordered registered.

Deed: Jesse Wolfe to Archelaus Branch for 293 acres, proved by Alexander Moris; Ordered registered.

Deed: Mark Rogers to Thomas Benett, Jr. for 102 acres, proved by Jesse Gulley; Ordered registered.

Deed: Martin Hanchy to Isaac James for 212 acres, Acknowledged; Ordered registered.

Deed: Samuel Davis to Lewis Smith for 69 acres, Acknowledged; Ordered registered.

Deed: Joseph Thomas Rhodes to William Nethercut for 75 acres, proved by Nathan Waller; Ordered registered.

Deed: James Venters to Daniel Boyet for 150 acres, proved by James Boyet; Ordered registered.

Deed: Matthew Ward to Bryan Whitfield for 266 acres, Acknowledged; Ordered registered.

Deed: John Williams to Joseph Williams for 2 pieces of land 52 pieces of land [sic], proved by David Williams; Ordered registered.

Deed: William Gore to Lewis Carleton for 100 acres, proved by Joseph Bray; Ordered registered.

Deed: Jacob Mainor to James Williams for 2 pieces of land, 270 acres, proved by Burrell Williams; Ordered registered.

Deed: Jehu Cook to Reuben Norris for 200 acres, proved by Isom Norris; Ordered registered.

Deed: James Raphel to Sampson Grimes for 2 pieces of land, 112 acres, proved by John Best; Ordered registered.

Deed: James Kenan to William Browning for 285 acres, Acknowledged; Ordered registered.

Deed: James Kenan to Martin Wells for 285 acres, Acknowledged; Ordered registered.

Deed: Lewis Barfield to Lucrecia Barfield for 200 acres, proved by Owen O'Daniel; Ordered registered.

Deed: John Johnston to Andrew McIntire for 50 acres, Acknowledged; Ordered registered.

Deed: William Ezell to Lewis Carleton for 190 acres, Acknowledged; Ordered registered.

Deed: Archibald Parker to Robert Cole for 72 acres, proved
by Bird Lanier; Ordered registered.

Deed: Matthew Edwards to John Padget for 150 acres, proved
by John Hussey; Ordered registered.

Deed: Ezekiel Allen to Jehu Cook for 100 acres, proved by
Benjamin Bratcher; Ordered registered.

Deed: Isaac Bizzell to James Bizzell for 250 acres, proved
by Francis Oliver; Ordered registered.

Deed: Bryan Whitfield to Simon Herring for 200 acres, proved
by Edward Pearsall; Ordered registered.

Deed: Edward Armstrong to Andrew Thally for 300 acres, Acknowledged; Ordered registered.

Deed: James Hall, Sheriff to William Frederick for 175
acres, Acknowledged; Ordered registered.

Deed: James Hall to Isom Lanier for 2 pieces of land, 200
acres, proved by William Southerland; Ordered registered.

Deed: Margaret Murphy, Daniel Murphy, Sarah Murphy & Timothy
Murphy to Arthur Murray for 130 acres, proved by John Gilman;
  Ordered registered.

Deed: Charles Hooks & Auston Bryan to William Pickett for 3
pieces of land, proved by Hugh McCanne; Ordered registered.

Deed: William Alberson to James Summerlin for 50 acres,
proved by Michael Glisson; Ordered registered.

A further account of Sale of Estate of Edward Dickson, dec'd,
rendered by Jehu Wilkinson, Adm'r; Ordered registered.

Ordered Grand Jury have Tickets for one day this Term.

Ordered Petit Jury have Tickets for two days each this Term:
Robert Sloan, William Kornegay, John Gilman, Edward Winders,
Daniel Kenan, Stephen Brown, James Winders, Isom Norris,
Tobias Southerland, William Hall, David Wright & Samuel
Davis.

Following appointed Jurymen to next Court: David Midleton,
Jehu Wilkinson, Andrew McIntire, Hogan Hunter, Isaac Midleton, William McGowen, Edward Pearsall, Jr., Howell Best,

John Neal, John Maxwell, Frederick Smith, Jr., John Houston,
Matthew Ward, Thomas Dale, Bryan Glisson, Simeon Garner,
Stephen Jones, Bazill Kornegay, John Watkins, John Beck,
William Burnham, John Wilkinson, Alex'r Herring, James
Rhodes, John Carleton, Thomas Wells, John Stallings, Joseph
Hodgeson, Shad'k Stallings, Jr., John Carr, Joseph Williams,
Richard James, Stephen Williams, Henry Fountain, Thomas Cole,
Jacob Lanier, James Pickett, Jr., Bryan Farrior, Jacob Brown,
Jr.

William Dickson, Clerk of this County Court, delivered to
Court 22 Books, being the Acts of Congress for 1802 & 1803,
which Books are deposited in hands of John Hunter near the
Court House.

Mr. Hunter is directed to let them out to such persons who
wish to read them & who are to return them to him again in
Six Months & no Person is to have more than two at one time.
William Beck has received two of them.

Appointed Lewis Hall & James Chambers Patrollers in District
of Capt. Bests Co.

Appointed Edward Pearsall, Andrew McIntire & Jehu Wilkinson a
Committee to settle accounts of the Orphans of Charles Brown,
dec'd, with Thomas Findley their Guardian & return a correct
statement to next Court.

A Plan of the division of 290 acres of Estate of Jacob Kornegay, dec'd, was submitted by the Committee appointed to
divide same between the three claimants, Penelope, Henry &
Mary Kornegay, The Court laid it over until next Court for
further information upon a suggestion that some of the lines
thereof have been extended beyond the limits of the Patent
thereof.

The Court Adjourned Till Court in Course.

[signed] J. Pearsall, Ja'b Williams, William Southerland,
Edw'd Pearsall.

Minutes of April Term 1805 which were not entered before the
Dockett was signed:

Ordered following Justices appointed to take lists of
Taxables for this year:
   For Capt. Herrings Co. - James Wright, Esq.
   For Capt. Watkins Co. - Bryan Bowden, Esq.
   For Capt. J. Swinsons Co. - Jo Whitfield, Esq.

       For Capt. J. A. Swinsons Co. - Isaac Kornegay, Esq.
       For Capt. Houstons Co. - Jacob Williams, Esq.
       For Capt. Browns Co. - W. Southerland, Esq.
       For Capt. Mannings Co. - Ben. Lanier, Esq.
       For Capt. Carrs Co. - Tim. Teachy, Esq.
       For Capt. Blands Co. - D. Williams, Esq.
       For Capt. Wells Co. - Gibson Sloan, Esq.
       For Capt. Midletons Co. - James Dickson, Esq.
       For Capt. Beats Co. - Edward Pearsall, Esq.

    Ordered Clerk issue Certificates for the above appointments
    as Law directs.

    Signed by James Maxwell, W. Southerland, C. Hooks, H.
    McCanne, J. Pearsall, Joseph T. Rhodes, Edw'd Pearsall;
    Test: Wm Dickson, CC

10 May 1805 Special Court held at the Court House for Special
    purpose of trying a Negro man Slave Jim, the property of
    Lewis Barfield, Prossecuted by David Hooks for threatening to
    take the life of a Negro man named Lam, the property of said
    David.

    The Justices & Jury Convened by Sheriff: Edward Pearsall,
    James Dickson & Hugh McCanne, Esquires, Justices, Felix
    Frederick, Thomas Sheppard, Maurice Fennell, William Hall,
    William Stoakes, William Pickett, Mesheck Stallings, George
    Houston, Jonathan Thomas, David Wright, John Hall, John
    Houston.

    James Hall, Esq., Sheriff of the County, returned the Warrant
    with the said Negro Jim in Custody, The Warrant being in the
    following words:

       State of North Carolina, Duplin County. David Hooks
       complains on Oath that he has reason to believe that
       the life of his Negro man Lamb is in Danger of being
       taken by a Negro man Jim, the Property of Lewis Bar-
       field. You are therefore required to call assistants
       and take the Body of the said Jim and bring him before
       some Justice for said County to be dealt with as the
       law directs. Given under my hand this 8th day of May
       1805. [signed] Cha. Hooks
       Returned Executed. Signed, John Southerland.

    Parties appeared. Judgement that the Constable deliver the
    within named Jim to the Sheriff with directions to call a

Court of three Justices & freeholders to try him according to law. [signed] Cha. Hooks, 19th May 1805. Executed - James Hall, Sher.

The Jury sworn & witnesses Examined & Charges in Warrant fully proved, the Jury bro't in Verdict of Guilty; Court Ordered said Jim to receive on his bare back one hundred lashes, which Order was executed by the Sheriff.

Witnesses: Jehu Wilkinson, Cl'k pro tem.

Coppey of the Proceedings - Test: Wm. Dickson CC

15 July 1805 County Court begun & held for County of Duplin at the Court House, the third Monday.

Present: Worshipfull Edward Pearsall, Esq. who adjourned Court.

Tuesday Morning [16 Jul 1805] Court met at 9 o'clock according to adjournment.

Present: Worshipfull James Kenan, James Outlaw, Daniel Glisson & William Duncan, Esquires.

Ordered John Ward be Overseer of the road leading from Prospect Meeting House to Job Leary's & have following hands to work under him: Robert Irwin, Daniel Boyet, Isaac Dawson, Joseph Dawson, John Quinney, Benjamin Deaver, Alexander Deaver, James Stewart, Dan'l Stewart & Alexander Carter.

Appointed Joseph T. Rhodes, William Southerland & Jacob Williams, Esquires a Committee to settle accounts of Estate of Samuel Houston, dec'd with the Adm'rs & Reporte to next Court.

Grand Jury sworn: Jehu Wilkinson, foreman, Thomas Wells, Nathan Ward, John Wilkinson, Stephen Jones, Howell Best, Shadrack Stallings, Jr., David Midleton, James Pickett, Henry Fountain, Simeon Garner, Jacob Brown, Jr., Jacob Lanier, Thomas Cole, Hogan Hunter.

Ordered Thomas Evens, Constable, attend Grand Jury.

As Charles Mitchell, a Minor, was bound apprentice to Jesse Hardy till age 21 & it having been represented to this Court

that he has been ill treated by his said Master, Court Ordered said Charles Mitchell be liberated from said Indentures
& be put in possession of Robert Searl & Charles Creel[?]
both of Lenoir County where said Minor was brought from.

Ordered also that said Jesse Hardy be discharged from any
further care towards said Charles Mitchell.

Appointed Thomas Kenan, David Williams & William Stoakes a
Committee to settle accounts of Estate of Benjamin Byrd,
dec'd, with John Hufham, Adm'r & return same to Court.

Read Petition of Lewis Barfield praying a Renewal of a former
Order which he had to build a Public Grist Mill on Burncoat
Swamp where the Road crosses it & where he is the owner of
land on both sides of said Run & where he has begun said
work; Ordered said former Order continued & he have leave to
finish said Mill.

William Brown & Jacob Monk, appointed Patrollers at July
Term, 1804 and having served for Term of one year are allowed
40 shillings each for said service.

Appointed Daniel Glisson, Esq. Overseer of the River in room
of Isaac Kornegay & to have same District & hands: Fred'k
Smith, Jr., Jones Smith, Jesse Smith, Lawsons Tim, Alex'r
Graddys Peter, Jacob Williams Bob, Isaac Kornegays hands,
Samuel Smiths hands, Bryan Glisson & Daniel Glissons own
hands.

Reporte of Committee appointed to settle accounts of Estate
of Benjamin Byrd, dec'd, with John Hufham, Adm'r, Returned &
signed by said Committee by which it appears there is in
hands of said Adm'r £69-11-7; Court concurred & Ordered
recorded.

Ordered John Becks & Mark Rogers hands be taken off Road
where Thomas Wright is Overseer & ad[d]ed to John Becks
District in order to keep the path way open for Passage of
Carriages & Travellers from Mr. Sandifurs place into the
other old Road at the old School house above Jesse Millards &
that said hands work under said John Beck.

John Hufham, Abraham Newton, Aaron Williams & John Williams,
appointed Patrollers at July Term 1804, & served as such are
allowed 40 shillings each for said service.

Ordered Daniel Glisson, William Kornegay, Jr., Owen O'Daniel,
David Kornegay, Frederick Graddy, Lewis Barfield, Christopher
Lawson, Frederick Smith, Sr., Alex'r Graddy, Sr., Henry Grad-
dy, Frederick Graddy (Neuse), Lewis Barfield, Jr. & Jacob

Williams, Esq., or any 12, be a Jury to lay off to Sarah
Churchwell, widow of Wm. Churchwell, dec'd, her Dower &
Reporte to Court.

Appointed George Powell Overseer of the New Road laid off
from Benjamin Bradshaws to Murrays landing & have following
hands: Walter Bryan, Frederick Bowen, Nicanor Murray, John
Whitman, Jr., Benjamin Bradshaw, Jehu Cook, Edward Street,
William George, Fred'k George, James Carter & Joseph Hodgeson.

As James Midleton, Sr. was appointed Guardian to Kitty
Garrison, a Minor & the said James Midleton is dead, Court
appointed Thomas Garrison Guardian to said Kitty Garrison,
who has given Bond of £300; Ordered he take her Estate into
his possession.

Appointed Edmund Duncan a Constable, he gave Bond.

Appointed Elisha Gibbs Overseer of the Road in room of Bryan
Bowden & is to have same district & hands.

Read Petition of Sundry Inhabitants between the NorthEast &
Goshen praying a new Road leading from the NorthEast near
Outlaws Bridge to Cross the Beaverdam at Jonathan Keithleys &
from thence into the Road near Isaac Kornegays & that a Jury
be appointed to lay off said Road & reporte to next Court:
Ordered James Outlaw, Edward Outlaw, Jonathan Keithly,
["Daniel Glisson" marked through], Isaac Kornegay, Samuel
Goff, James Smyth, Samuel Smyth, Frederick Graddy, Alexander
Graddy, Davie Carter, Owen O'Daniel, David Kornegay, William
Kornegay, Sr., William Kornegay, Jr. & Alexander O'Daniel, or
any 12, be a Jury to lay off said New Road & Reporte to next
Court & that David Kornegay, Constable summon & convene &
Daniel Glisson, Esq. Qualifie said Jury.

Ordered Lemuel Cherry be allowed for service as Constable
20 shillings for each year he summoned Inhabitants of his
District to give in their lists of Taxables- ["it being 3
years" marked through] amounting to £3.

Petit Jury Qualified: John Houston - 2 days, Thomas Daile -
3 days, Alex'r Herring - 3 days, Fred'k Smith, Jr. - 1 day,
Bryan Farrior - 3 days, Isaac Midleton - 3 days, James Rhodes
- 3 days, John Maxwell - 3 days, Stephen Williams - 3 days,
William McGowen - 3 days, Bazil Kornegay - 3 days, Edward
Pearsall - 3 days, John T. Rhodes as Tallisman - 1 day.

Appointed John Connerly Overseer of Road in room of Owen
Connerly & to have same District & hands.

Appointed Benjamin Johnston Overseer of Road in room of William Pollock & to have same District & hands.

Nicanor Murray appointed Overseer of River in room of Nicanor James & to have same District & hands.

Nathan Waller appointed a Patroller in 1804 & served is allowed 40 shillings.

Appointed John McCanne Overseer of the River from Brocks Landing down to Indian Grave Bluff & following to work under him: Daniel Murphy, Enoch Parker, Dawson Pickett, Jeremiah Wallace, Andrew Wallace, John Pickett, Dan'l Murphys Negro Travis, Lincoln Shuffield, Thomas Cottle, Reuben Cottle.

Ordered said Overseer & hands clear out the Cut that is opened across below James Picketts that Boats may pass it without Danger.

Granted Adm'n of Estate of Hicks Mills to William Southerland who gave Bond of £1500 & took Oath of Adm'r.

Appointed James Gufford a Constable & he gave Bond.

Appointed Willis Hines a Constable & he gave Bond.

Appointed Samuel Herring a Constable & he gave Bond.

Appointed William Alberson Guardian to Jesse Ellison, Minor Orphan & he gave Bond of £500; Ordered he take his Estate into his possession.

Account of Sale of Estate of Michael Sullivan, dec'd, Exhibited by Milley Sullivan, Adm'x; Ordered recorded.

Reporte of Committee appointed to lay off to Sarah Churchwell one years provisions of her dec'd Husbands Estate Exhibited; Ordered recorded & filed.

Account of Sale of Estate of William Churchwell, dec'd, Exhibited by Sarah Churchwell, Adm'x; Ordered recorded & filed.

Inventory of Estate of James Gillespie, dec'd Exhibited by David Gillespie, Jo Gillespie, Ex'rs; Ordered recorded.

Account of Sale of Estate of James Gillespie, dec'd, amounting to $7,736.66; Ordered recorded & filed.

Last Will & Testament of James Midleton, dec'd, Exhibited & proved by Joseph Gillespie & Peter Frederick & at same time

David Midleton & Robert Midleton, Executors named in said
Will, Qualified.

Court proceeded to elect a Sheriff & unanimously elected
James Hall, Esquire; Ordered Clerk certifie same so
Commission may issue.

Wednesday Morning [17 Jul 1805] Court met at 9 o'clock
according to adjournment.

Present: Worshipfull James Kenan, Joseph T. Rhodes, Daniel
Glisson & James Maxwell, Esquires.

Ordered Ex'rs of James Midleton, dec'd, sell all that part of
said dec'd Estate not bequeathed in said dec'ds Will & return
same to next Court.

Appointed Inspecters of the Poll in holding the Ensuing Elec-
tions on the second Thursday in August next: At Hodges -
David Wright & Lewis Dickson, Federal; Thomas Wright &
William Beck, State; At Stanleys - William Duncan & John
Watkins, Federal; Henry Graddy & Edward Alberson, State; At
Bryans - Wm. Southerland & Sam'l Houston, Federal; Rob't
Southerland & John Houston, State; At D'd Williams - Aaron
Williams & John Hufham, Federal; Gibson Sloan & John Max-
well, State; At the Court House Second Friday in August,
James Dickson & Jehu Wilkinson, Federal; Thomas Routledge &
Joseph Gillespie, State.

Jehu Wilkinson, Edward Pearsall & Edward Armstrong appointed
a Committee to settle accounts of Estate of Isaac Hunter,
dec'd with Col. Charles Ward, Adm'r so as to ascertain the
share of said Estate due Isaac Hunter, one of the Claimants
& in the hands of said Charles Ward & return same to next
Court.

Upon Examination of a former Order in favor of Susana Carter
who had charged Bently Weston of being the father of a Bastard Child, it is found that Susana Carter has been allowed
against Bently Weston the sum of £26 in full of all demands
& that said Weston has produced Receipts for payment of
£12-10-0 of the said sum so that there is yet £13-10-0 due
said Susana Carter which when paid by said Weston will be in
full of all due her on that account.

Anna McGee, Widow of Holden McGee obtained Adm'n on Estate of
Holden McGee, dec'd & gave Bond of £500 & took Oath of Adm'x.
pd. 16/.

Amos Shuffield an Infirm man is exempted from working on the Roads in future.

Ordered Bently Stewart a Minor, bound Apprentice to James Stewart till age 21 to learn to Read the Bible & write & Cypher as far as the rule of three & the Trade of a Hatter.

Appointed William Cranford a Constable, he gave Bond.

Appointed William Matthews a Constable, he gave Bond.

George E. Houston, charged with begeting a Bastard child of Isabel Jones, a single woman, gave Bond required by Law.

James Stewart is appointed Overseer of the Road in room of Alexander Carter & to have same hands & that piece of the Old Road that leads from Sam'l Davis towards Outlaws bridge as far as the Edge of Edward Albersons District be ad[d]ed to his District of the New Road.

Appointed Bryan Farrior & ["Phil Southerland" marked through] Willis Bishop Patrollers in District of Capt. Browns Co.

Ordered County Surveyor with James Grimes, Joseph Whitfield & Stephen Jones be a Committee to ascertain the bounds of a 150 acres allotted to Martin Kornegay of his dec'd Fathers Estate including the Mill & Plantation & return to next Court.

Pursuant to an Order of last Court a Jury has been convened & laid off a New Road from the black River Road at Harvills Bay thence to a foard Crossing the Doctors Creek near Abraham Newkirks & from thence into a Road leading to South Washington; Court concurred & Ordered Brittain Powell be Overseer of said Road & that Daniel Alderman, Jr., Elias Sutton, David Alderman, Jr., Enoch Newton, Isaac Newton, Jesse Lee, Joshua Lee, James Newton, Elisha Powell, William Hysmith, John Alderman, William Roades, William Bland, Joseph Stringfield, Richard Welsh, Elijah Powell, William White & John Smith work under him.

Appointed David Hooks, Isham Faison & John Connerly Patrollers in Capt. Herrings Co.

Pursuant to an Order passed July Term, 1804 to turn the Road from James Armstrongs fence to a Swamp called Reedy Meadow, A Jury has laid off same; Ordered same be considered a Public Road.

As at last Court a Petition from Sundry Inhabitants on the heads of Rockfish praying for a New Road laid off leading

from Main Road at Harvilla Bay the most direct way into the
Main Road at John Williams was Granted; Ordered Thomas Goff,
John Hufham, Abraham Newton, Jacob Newton, Edw'd Bowen, John
Wilson, Jonathan Willis, Joseph Williams, David Davis, Samuel
Davis, Richard Blanton, Stephen Williams be a Jury to lay off
said New Road & report a Plan thereof before the next Court.

Ordered Abraham Newton be Overseer of said New Road & have
the following hands: John Lee, John Wilson, Thomas Goff,
William Devane, Samuel Beck, Abraham Bell, Martha Bells
hands, Uriah Suggs, John Hufham, Edward Bowen, Abraham Newton, Joseph Williams, David Williams, Samuel Davis, Richard
Blanton, James Young, Henry Cook, Samuel West, Lewis Smyth &
James Blanton.

["John Wilkinson is appointed Overseer of the Road in room of
William McGowen & have same District & hands" marked out.]

Ordered Thomas Cottle Sited to next Court to show cause why
Execution should not issue against him for maintinence of a
Bastard Child begotten by him of Sarah Johnston, for £12
which Court has adjudged against him.

Granted petition of William Alberson to turn the Road round
his fence with Proviso that William Alberson do open & make
good said Road to the satisfaction of Overseer & hands on
said Road.

Reporte of Settlement of Accounts of Estate of Charles Brown,
dec'd, with Thomas Findley, Guardian of Orphans of said
dec'd, Exhibited by Committee appointed; Court concurred &
Ordered recorded.

By above reporte it is stated they find in hands of said
Guardian a ballance due said Orphans of £416-14-5 1/4.

Additional Sale of Estate of Benj'n Byrd, dec'd, amounting to
£8-4-6 Exhibited by John Hufham, Adm'r; Ordered Recorded.

Thursday Morning [18 Jul 1805] Court met at 9 o'clock according
to adjournment.

Present: Worshipfull James Kenan, James Outlaw, Shadrack
Stallings, Edward Pearsall, James Maxwell, Charles Hooks,
Esquires.

Peter Frederick & Felix K. Hill appointed Patrollers for 1804
& having served as such are allowed each 40 shillings for
said service.

Edward Pearsall, Jr. appointed a Patroller for 1804 & having
served as such is allowed 40 shillings for said service.

Joseph Gillespie appointed a Patroller at July Term 1804 &
having served as such is allowed 40 shillings for said
service.

Continued William McGowen Overseer of the Road as formerly &
the following hands to work under him: his own hands, Watson
Burtons, James Fredericks, John Hunters, John Wilkinsons &
Widow James (X Roads).

Appointed Phill Southerland a Constable, he gave Bond.

Deed: Felix K. Hill to James Winders for 84 acres, proved by
Charles Hooks; Ordered registered.

Deed of Gift: Charles Hooks to his three children, Betsey
Jean, Kitty & Narcissa for three Negroes, Acknowledged;
Ordered registered.

Deed: Edward Armstrong to Thomas Shoalar for 84 acres,
Acknowledged; Ordered registered.

Deed: Arthur Pitman to Hosea Pitman for sundries proved by
William Pickett; Ordered registered.

Deed: Jacob Parker to Nath'l McCanne for sundries, proved by
John Devaul; Ordered registered.

Bill of Sale: Jacob Parker to Nathaniel McCanne for a horse,
proved by James Williams Williams [sic] & Merit Manning;
Ordered registered.

Deed: Jacob Williams to John & Outlaw Williams for 435
acres, proved by Edward Pearsall; Ordered registered.

Deed: Jacob Williams to his Children for sundry Goods &
Chattels, proved by Edward Pearsall; Ordered registered.

Quit Claim Deed: David Brock to Leven Watkins for 100 acres,
proved by Hezekiah Millard; Ordered registered.

Deed: Hugh McCanne, Sheriff to Auston Bryan for 70 acres,
Acknowledged; Ordered registered.

Deed: David Brock to George Brice for 220 acres, proved by
Henry Newkirk; Ordered registered.

Deed: David Brock to Abraham Newkirk for 99 acres, proved by
Henry Newkirk; Ordered registered.

Deed: Gideon Arthur to William Pickett for 160 acres, Acknowledged; Ordered registered.

Deed: James Hall, Sheriff to Henry Cannon for 284 acres,
proved by Samuel Russell Jocelyn; Ordered registered.

Deed: Elizabeth Taylor & John Taylor to Jacob Taylor for 75
acres, proved by Benjamin Hodges; Ordered registered.

Deed: Frederick Wells to William Brown for 35 acres, Acknowledged; Ordered registered.

Deed: Daniel Murphy to Thomas Garrison for 58 acres, proved
by David Brock; Ordered registered.

Deed: Jacob Johnston to William Bowden[?] for 91 acres,
proved by Archibald Thomas; Ordered registered.

Deed: John Holden to Asa Murray for 410 acres, proved by
Thomas E. James; Ordered registered.

Deed of Gift: Charles King to Elenor Kinnard for a Negro,
Acknowledged; Ordered registered.

Deed of Gift: Joseph Sandifer to James Kinnard, proved by
Charles King; Ordered registered.

Deed: Nathaniel Price to David Dural for 80 acres, proved by
Bazill Kornegay; Ordered registered.

Deed: Benjamin Rhodes to Samuel Whaley for 16 1/2 acres,
proved by Joseph T. Rhodes; Ordered registered.

Deed: George Kornegay Jr. & Betsey Kornegay to John Kornegay
for 125 acres, proved by George Duncan; Ordered registered.

Deed: John Beck to Joseph Kornegay for 500 acres, Acknowledged; Ordered registered.

Deed: Thomas Johnston to Benjamin Johnston for 505 acres,
proved by James Reardon; Ordered registered.

Deed: Thomas Johnston to Joseph Johnston for 200 acres,
proved by James Reardon; Ordered registered.

Deed: Nathan Fountain to Robert Cole for 175 acres, proved
by Henry Fountain; Ordered registered.

Bill of Sale: John Goff to Thomas Garrison for a Negro Wench
Emmey, proved by John Carr; Ordered registered.

Deed: David Gillespie to Joseph Gillespie for lands in State of Tennessee, proved by James Rowland; Ordered registered.

Appointed Jehu Wilkinson, Edward Pearsall & James Hall a Committee to settle accounts of Estate of Kitty Molten, now Kitty Peacock with John McGowen her Guardian & return same to next Court.

Appointed Hezekiah Millard, Benjamin Bowden, Samuel Herring & George Duncan Patrollers in District of Capt. Winders Co.

Appointed following Jurymen to next Court: William McGee, Thomas Sheppard, Gabriel James, Thomas McGee, James McGowen, Benjamin Brown, Andrew McIntire, John Connerly, William Frederick, Jr., William Pollock, Elias Faison, Andrew Hurst, Benjamin Bowden, Edward Winders, Jesse Swinson, James Jernigan, Sam'l Smyth, Archelaus Branch, William Mainor, Henry Newkirk, Lewis Davis, Nathan Waller, James Lanier, Sr., Dawson Pickett, John Fountain, John Neale, Jeremiah Pearsall, Benj'n Best, John Carr, Joseph Hodgeson, Asa Murray, John Carleton, ["William Stoakes" marked out], Joseph Brice, Amos Shuffield, Joseph Williams, Richard James, Dan'l Alderman, Jr., Richard Swinson, Stephen Martindell & James Holland.

Appointed Joseph T. Rhodes, Esq., Nathan Waller & John Farrior a Committee to lay off to Elizabeth Mills the Widow of Hicks Mills, dec'd, one years provisions for herself & family or the value thereof & return same to next Court.

Ordered same Committee to divide the Negro property of Estate of Hicks Mills, dec'd, between Claimants & return same to next Court.

Ordered Adm'r of Hicks Mills, dec'd, sell Estate of dec'd & return same to next Court.

Allowed Thomas Evens 16/ for attending Court two days this Term.

Allowed Merrit Maning & Phill Southerland 16/ each for attending two days as Constable this Term.

Ordered Grand Jury men have Tickets for two days each this Term & Petit Jury for three days or according to their service who were of the Venieri.

Court Adjourned Till Court in Course.

[signed] Edw'd Pearsall, Hugh McCanne, W. Southerland.

General Index

HEATH (cont.)
  John...................44
  Levi...................76
  Thomas.........34(2),45(2),
    51,55,59
  William................76
  Wm.....................76
HEDLET[?]
  Senea..................12
HENDERSON
  Nancy...................9
HERRING
  Alex'r.................83,87
  Alexander..............69,74
  Benjamin...............18,27
  Capt.....6,12,17,41,44,83,90
  David...................8
  Elisha.................27,69
  Lewis..........7,39,40,74
  Lewis, Esq.............17
  Mrs....................69
  Sam'l..................68
  Samuel......32,39,40(5),62,
    74,88,94
  Simon..................82
  Stephen......15,28,38(4),39,
    40,41(2),47(2),61,69
  Stephen B.....10,12,38,39(3)
  Stephen Bright.........38(4)
  Stephen (M)............21
  Stephen (Mill).........51
  Stephen Mill...........18
  Whitfield..............41
  Widow..................69(2)
HEWIT[?]
  Andrew.................17
HICKS
  Charles, Esq...........11
  Lewis..................60
HIGGINS
  William.......42,43,60,61,80
HILL
  Felix K....16,44,51,62,91,92
  Felix Kenan............15
  John...................3,19
  John Hatch.............53
  John, Jr................3
  Thomas.................10,12
  William.......3(2),11(2),33,
    36,53,59,67
HINES
  Elinor.................67
  Joel...................30

HINES (cont.)
  Marrinna [Marianna].......72
  Stephen...................72
  Willis.......7,27,42,64,65,
    71,76,88
HOBSON
  Henry......................5
HODGES
 89
  Ben.......................42
  Benj'n.................60,69
  Benjamin........42,49,69,93
HODGESON
  Aaron.....................62
  Joseph..........57,83,87,94
HODOM
  G. J.......................4
  Geo. Jernigan.........2,4,5
  George J..................68
HOLDEN
  John.........11,30(2),59,93
HOLLAND
  Daniel....................59
  James.....................94
HOLLINGSWORTH
  Henry.....................70
  William.......4,45,51,57,70
  Wm........................65
HOOKS
  Betsey Jean...............92
  C.........................84
  Cha...............62,84,85
  Cha., Esq.................65
  Charles....8(2),13,25(2),32,
    34,37,47,62,63(2),65(2),
    75,82,92(2)
  Charles, Esq..3(2),11,13,19,
    35,41,45,54,75,91
  David........12,22,49,54,61,
    62,84(3),90
  Hillary...............62,77
  James.....................62
  Kitty.....................92
  Narcissa..................92
  Susana....................22
  Thomas...............7,22(3)
HOUSTON
  Anna......................74
  Capt............41,52,78,84
  Edward.............39,50,79
  George...7,12,27,37,41,68,84
  George E...........49(2),90
  Henry.....................37

Geographical Index

www.ingramcontent.com/pod-product-compliance
Lightning Source LLC
Chambersburg PA
CBHW021835020426
42334CB00014B/634